Dear Boy, Dear Girl

Dear Boy, Dear Girl

AN ANTHOLOGY OF LETTERS WRITTEN
TO CHILDREN AND YOUNG PEOPLE
UP TO SIXTEEN YEARS OF AGE

COLLECTED AND EDITED BY

Mavis Norrie

CONSTABLE · LONDON

First published in Great Britain 1998
by Constable and Company Ltd
3 The Lanchesters, 162 Fulham Palace Road
London W6 9ER
Copyright © 1998 Mavis Norrie
ISBN 0 09 479190 2
Set in Monotype Garamond by
Servis Filmsetting Ltd, Manchester
Printed in Great Britain by
St Edmundsbury Press Ltd
Bury St Edmunds, Suffolk

A CIP catalogue record for this book
is available from the British Library

To my beloved 'Henry',

Thank you for our family,
Thank you for my life

'. . . Letters . . . should be familiar conversations between
absent friends . . .'

Lord Chesterfield

CONTENTS

ACKNOWLEDGEMENTS

I should like to thank Priscilla Jaretski, the first person to whom I spoke of my plan for this anthology and who responded with a burst of enthusiasm that yielded several writers; Lyte M. Fozard, professional researcher recommended by the Library of Congress, Washington, DC, whose reaction was dynamic and who provided me with quantities of material enabling me to give the book a welcome transatlantic flavour; Mary Lutyens (Mrs J.G. Links) and her niece Candia Petersen who kindly gave me access to hitherto unpublished letters; Joan Aiken who gave me similar letters relating to her family; Barbara Scott who researched on my behalf at the Imperial War Museum; Peggy Bowyer who carried out various essential commissions; and the late Michael Floyd who illustrated the letter to my grandchildren, at my request.

I should also like to thank the following for suggesting letters, lending and giving me books, helping me prepare the typescript and expressing their support for my project: the late Edward Blishen, Ruth Elliott, Margaret Forster, Inge Hyman, Jessica Norrie, Marianne Obey, Maureen Paterson, Wendy Trewin, Christopher Wade and those many librarians in municipal libraries and at the London Library, who helped me professionally – especially the two jolly men from Enfield in their mobile trailer.

My thanks to my daughter Amanda, for indefatigable secretarial work, editorial advice and encouragement, to her and her husband Gerald Leversha, for putting the entire book on their computer, not once but several times and lastly to my husband, Ian, who encouraged and enthused at every stage. Then, when called upon, he undertook essential but unglamorous administrative and sub-editorial duties for which I am truly grateful.

The compiler acknowledges with thanks permissions granted by the undermentioned persons, companies, institutions, to quote from the works indicated:

The Trustees of the C.L. Dodgson Estate and A.P. Watt Ltd for the *Letters of Charles Dodgson & Lewis Carroll*, edited by Morton Cohen; Roger Nicholls for the *Debussy Letters*, ed. Nichols & Lesure; Lady Mollie Butler for the letter from Lady Ann Butler; The National Trust and A.P. Watt Ltd for *O Beloved Kids*: Letters from Kipling to his children; Cambridge University Press and Laurence Pollinger Ltd for the letter to Harwood Brewster from *The Letters of D.H. Lawrence Vol 6, 1927–8*; HarperCollins for *Letters to Children* by C.S. Lewis; The Broadlsands Archives for the letter from Lady Milfordhaven in Philip Ziegler's *Mount-Batten*; Judy Taylor and Frederick Warne & Co for the letter from Beatrix Potter to Winifred Warne in *Letters to Children from Beatrix Potter*; HarperCollins for the *Letters of J.R.R. Tolkien*; Random House and Martin Secker & Warburg for *Swing hammer swing!* by Jeff Torrington; The Orion Publishing Group and George Weidenfeld & Nicolson for *The Letters of Kenneth Tynan* ed. Kathleen Tynan, and for *The Letters of Evelyn Waugh*, ed. Mark Amory; Random House and the Hogarth Press for *Congenial Spirits*, the Letters of Virginia Woolf, edited by Nigel Nicolson & Janet Trautman Banks; Mrs. E.J. Grisenthwaite for the photograph and letters of Capt. James Foulis; Macmillan General Books for *Last Letters Home* ed. Tamasin Day Lewis; Hugh Bedford for picture letters by Frank Gascoigne Heath; Olive Davies for letters from her father, Mr. Lumley; Random House and Hutchinson for *Yours Plum*, the Letters of P.G. Wodehouse ed. Donaldson, and Her Majesty the Queen for the portrait of Elizabeth I when Princess, From the Royal Collection.

Every effort has been made to contact certain other persons and publishers where it was believed permission should be sought. Where no replies have been received and material used the compiler acknowledges her indebtedness and wishes to express her willingness to pay a reproduction fee if required.

MAVIS NORRIE

PREFACE

'How would it be,' I thought, 'to make a collection of letters written to children?' And then: 'How old is a child?'

It took only a moment to decide that my 'children' must be no older than sixteen. Never mind the technicalities, the vote, the school-leaving age, the ages of consent. The very words – sixteen, seventeen – suggest what they are. Sixteen is the sound of footsteps on the early morning frost. Seventeen is already moving gracefully towards the terrace to join the adults under the sunshades.

Lord Chesterfield I discovered lends substance to these rather nebulous notions of mine. He addresses his son Philip as 'Dear Boy' until the 'boy' turns seventeen and becomes 'My dear young friend'. The collection, then, owes half its title to the Earl of Chesterfield, while for the other half we could go to a Dr Gregory of Edinburgh who posthumously and with coy enthusiasm exhorts his 'Dear Girls' not to lose their delectable ability to blush.

I discovered that in 1938 an American lady named Mrs Eva G. Connor published an admirable anthology of letters addressed to the same age group and called it, simply, *Letters to Children*. I have gratefully included a few of these.

But the book, I thought, would not be limited to the very young simply because of a little difficulty over the title. If it were, we should not hear any authentic adult voice. It would always be muffled in an extra gentleness, a specially adapted humour, a tentative approach.

That the recipients of these letters I chose had to be no older than sixteen is the only restriction placed upon the selection here. The only one, but it is severe, and obviously one regrets much good material that is lost. I do have a weakness for letters which give advice on how to write. Just possibly C.S. Lewis's letter to 'Joan' is written to a young woman of seventeen, but the counsel it gives is so interesting and practical that I wanted to pass it on. He is extremely good on adjectives. And there is another probable exception at the very end (p. 243).

The search for the letters was full of surprises. I thought some, even many, would be homilies, and that is so. But I expected every admonition, reproach or lecture to be delivered gently, with affection or humour, or both. Many are. When Rudyard Kipling had something particularly solemn to say to his children he invited a character to do it for him: 'Mr Campbell says, would you please . . .'

But consider the very first letter that I found (p. 35). It was from Lady Hamilton to her daughter Horatia, aged fourteen. Such a bad-tempered letter – nor was it for her, one cannot help feeling, to scold in that particular way. In fact, it is an injustice to represent Emma by this nasty little note, for she had been a marvellous letter-writer, exuberant, full of zest for life, and with a totally disarming enthusiasm for her own person and performance.

And what a harsh letter Jack London wrote to his elder daughter Joan (p. 157). His marriage having broken down several years before, he now wants Joan to make some kind of choice between her mother and himself. Joan replies, and this is the answer she gets. What a letter to send to a thirteen-year-old.

Sometimes one wonders whether the humour in these letters can always have been appreciated by the younger correspondents. There is a solemn piece of art criticism in a letter from the German writer Theodor Fontane to his son aged six, who had sent him a drawing. This is a delicious letter, but it must have bewildered the little boy (though delighting the mother).

One wonders, too, what six-year-old Storm (that was his nickname: he was born in a storm) Moulton Barrett made of that remarkable letter his sister Elizabeth sent him on standing up for one's principles (p. 42). A sustained, totally mature piece of satire coming from the pen of a girl of fifteen, it depicts the execution of a certain Master Storm Barrett and his calm and heroic behaviour on the occasion. Did the poor child have to be comforted and told that 'it was only Ba's fun'?

Sometimes it is the non-writers who have the knack of communicating with the young better, or at least as well as, one feels, the professionals. General Eisenhower wrote a perfect little letter to his niece Ruthie, aged three (in 1943: how did he turn his eyes long enough from current affairs just then?) To make an extra paragraph out of last year's blue dress was a master-stroke. Even if Ruthie had forgotten it herself, he recreated it for her and used it to make her feel important.

Kipling the great story-teller gives an amusing account of his investiture at Oxford University. Louisa May Alcott has provided a description of a newsboys' hostel. But I don't know that they do any better than Marianne Thornton, a woman of little formal education, describing to her great-nephew, E.M. Forster, the state opening of Parliament by George III to which she had been an eye-witness.

Certain letters took me by surprise. There were unexpected contrasts. Between two nieces, for example. Gustave Flaubert's – a horrid, cold girl, who showed no feeling for her uncle or his books except, after he died, to make a 'shrine' for him in the south of France – and, for herself, a lot of money. And D.H. Lawrence's who also created a shrine but with genuine devotion. She remembers the man with affection and reveres his work. She can tell you which poems are about what, and on what page of which edition you will find them. And here is John Keats, with another contrast: between the bright morning of his life, the family affection, the loving, *properly* ambitious parents – and the final horror in Rome, where the romantic poet dies unromantically, like Lawrence, from consumption.

Incidentally, it is lovely to hear Lawrence, the great and famous, once notorious, novelist, referred to as 'Uncle Bert'; as it is to hear of Kenneth Tynan in his self-styled role of 'loving Daddy'.

I soon gave up the struggle to keep any writer's 'quota' down to one or two letters. Nor have I enjoyed cutting letters. Very long letters, however, have clearly had to be omitted or shortened, so given here is only a tiny part of the letter Arthur Ashe wrote to his little daughter, Camera, for her to read after his death. But it is important not to eliminate the common humanity of these documents. Edward Moulton

Barrett's letter to three-year-old Elizabeth is frankly boring; but it is the first written communication in this famous father/daughter duo, and it tells us much about the preoccupations and responsibilities of this very young man at the time. The 'dull' bits often set the scene.

One fictional example is included. As Prologue there is Jeff Torrington's letter To an Unpublished Child which comes near the end of his first, and prize-winning novel, *Swing hammer swing!*

The letters are arranged mostly in chronological order according to the date of the writer's first letter. However, the correspondences of Queen Victoria and her family, and that of the Moulton Barretts, have been put into groups, as have letters from the First and Second World Wars. In the case of the Moulton Barretts, all references to Elizabeth Moulton Barrett, who was to become Elizabeth Barrett Browning, have been given as EBB. Idiosyncrasies of spelling and grammar have, in all cases, been retained as in the original letters.

If the book has a theme, it is to illustrate the immensely diverse ways in which people attempt to communicate with young people. I did not mean to reach a conclusion but themes have a way of emerging however varied the material. It became apparent that many of these letter writers were, in their different ways, attempting to instruct, educate or provide a moral foundation for the young recipients, and I was fascinated to observe the changes of approach over five hundred years. (Compare Martin Luther (p. 4) with Joan Aiken (p. 243).)

But not all the letters have a moral and my motives in putting them together were to entertain, intrigue and move some readers to find out more about the fascinating writers. There is much to laugh at, certainly tears to be shed, but most of all there is love.

PROLOGUE

To an unpublished child

JEFF TORRINGTON (b. 1935)

writer

Jeff Torrington, an artisan, won the Whitbread prize in 1992 with his first novel, *Swing hammer swing!* It is told in the first person by Tam Clay, an unemployed resident of Glasgow's Gorbals district. Tam's narrative spans a week's boozing during which his pregnant girl friend goes into hospital. He is reluctantly struck by the need to reform and ends the week by writing a letter to their 'unpublished child'.

Dear notyet,

Today, take my word for it, you're already heavier than a deluxe volume of *War and Peace*, and displaying such a sinuous complexity of purpose as to rival that opus. There, I knew you'd be pleased. Better still, your tests reveal your remarkable inventive vigour, not to mention your verve'n vivacity (Daddy has sent these v's flying like seabirds to brighten up his craggy prose). It would seem that the passing of your Homo sapiens exam is now a mere formality. Mammy and I are so proud of how you buckled down to your prelimbs. What a thrill the other day when Mammy let me touch a secret spot and I was able to feel the vibrations from that genetic typewriter you pound away at night'n day. An expert on your heroic little terranauts was able by means of a trumpetlike instrument to hear the most promising echoes from your 'wee blood beater' as he so drolly called it.

Things this side of the womb are so-so. Yeah, I'll straightshoot with you, they could be a whole wedge better. But don't you go bothering your bald wee bonce about anything: Daddy'll have a nifty wee nest all fixed up for your arrival. February's such a waste of a month: 'Snaw'n slush'n the lavvies'll no flush', as Mr Scobie puts it, so your advent will be all the more welcomed.

Since you've the inside gen you'll know that Mammy is doing fine although now'n again she gets to feeling a bit clunk. Not to worry, things'll work out, you'll see. So, just you away for a wee paddle in your dusky brook and let me do the worryin.

Keep up the good work.

Love, Daddy xxxxx

SIR THOMAS MORE (1478–1535)

Lord Chancellor of England and author

Thomas More, son of a judge, studied law and also devoted some years to prayer and contemplation before becoming a deeply loving family man. Henry VIII, on the recommendation of Cardinal Wolsey, appointed him to various high offices. When Wolsey fell from power, More reluctantly replaced him as Lord Chancellor. He subsequently refused to accept the King as head of the English Church and was sentenced to death for high treason.

More had four children by Jane, his first wife. This letter was written to them from Flanders (where his *Utopia* was originally published) in 1515. Margaret was by then about fourteen. (The original was in Latin; the translation echoes the rhythm of the Latin metre.)

[1515]

T. More sends greetings to his dearest children Margaret, Elisabeth, Cecily and John.

This one letter, designed to reach all four of my children,
Carries a father's wish thus to preserve them from ill.
Still as I plod on my way, and am drenched to the skin by the rain-storms,
Still as my labouring horse frequently sticks in the mud,
This is the verse that I make for you in the midst of my hardships,
Hoping that you may be pleased, rough as I know it to be.
This is a proof to you all of your father's love, for it shows you
How much dearer are you e'en than the sight of his eyes,
Since, though the ground may be soft and a tempest roaring around him,
Though the wee horse that he rides flounders afloat at the fords,

Still he cannot be torn from you, but in constant affection
Proves he remembers you well, no matter where he may be.
Even the threat of a fall with his horse, who frequently stumbles,
Sees him resolved to persist, pondering line upon line.
Verse comes hard for some who have much more leisure than I have,
Yet my fatherly love duly provides a supply.
    It's no wonderful thing if my heart embraces you wholly,
Thinking with awe as I do, 'I am the source of their life.'
Wise was old Nature of old, who linked man close to his offspring,
Joining their souls in a bond wrought with Herculean power.
Here is the source, do you see? of my mind's known tender indulgence,
Prone upon least excuse softly to fondle you all.
Here is why cake looms large in my thoughts of you, which are frequent,
Why fine pears (apples, too) figure as favourite gifts,
Why I so often have dressed you in silks, in Cathaian refulgence,
Why, too, the sight of your tears weakens my sternest resolves.
Well you know how often I kissed you, how rarely I spanked you,
– Yes, with a peacock's tail doing its best as a whip!
And, what is more, it was wielded in light soft blows, with compunction
Lest it should leave but a bruise scoring a tender behind.
Ah, what a beast is the man, unworthy the name of a father,
Who, when his children weep, weeps not in instant response!
Others may do as they will, but you are aware – and profoundly –
How in my dealings with you I show affectionate care.
All of my children alike have I loved with eagerness always,
And, as a father should be, I have been light on the rein:
Yet in amazement I find that love to have yielded an increase
Such that I seem to myself not to have loved you before.
This is because you have shown sage ways unlooked for in younglings,
This is because of your hearts, soundly and worthily formed,
This is because your speech is carefully trained in pronouncing,
This is because of your words, ordered and carefully weighed.
Nay I am so given up to my heart's irresistible yearning,
Now so enslaved to you all, pledges of mutual love,
Scarce does the mere stark fact of fleshly paternity move me,
Though of so many men's love that is the total and sum.
So, belovedest tribe of my offspring, straitly continue;
With your accustomed wiles strive to propitiate me,

And since your own good traits now deeply engage my affections,
So that I seem to myself not to have loved you before,
Let those traits (for they can) persuade my fondness hereafter,
So that I then may seem not to be loving you now.

MARTIN LUTHER (1483–1546)

German leader of the Protestant Reformation; priest, university lecturer and professor

Luther, a miner's son, was born at Eisleben. He graduated from Erfurt university in 1505. Two years later he was ordained and became a professor at Wittenberg university. In 1510–11 he visited Rome and was so appalled by the state of affairs at the Vatican that he wrote a thesis about the sale of papal indulgences and nailed it to a church door in Wittenberg. The hammer blows can still be heard.

Luther's books were banned and burned; he was tried for heresy, at Augsburg, and imprisoned. (Whilst in prison he began translating the Bible into German.) He married an ex-nun, in 1525, and had five children. This letter was written, about the time of his trial, to his eldest son, Hans, aged four. Lippus and Jost were Hans's siblings.

22 April 1530

To my dear son, Hans Luther: Grace and peace in Christ, my darling little son. I am very glad to hear that you are studying well and praying diligently. Go on doing so, my little son, and when I come home I will bring you a beautiful present.

I know a lovely, pretty garden, where there are many children. They wear golden coats, and pick up fine apples, pears, cherries, and plums under the trees. They sing and jump and are very merry. They also have beautiful little horses with bridles of gold and saddles of silver. I asked the man who owned the garden who the children were. He answered, 'These are the children who gladly pray and study and are good.' Then I said, 'Dear man, I also have a son named Hans Luther. Wouldn't he like to come into the garden and eat such beautiful apples and pears and ride such fine horses and play with these children!' Then the man said, 'If he prays and studies gladly, and is good, he too shall come into the garden, and Lippus and Jost with him. And when they are all here they shall have whistles and drums and lutes, and all sorts of things to make music with, and they shall dance and shoot with little crossbows.' And he showed me a beautiful meadow in the garden fixed for dancing. Gold whistles were hung there, and drums and silver crossbows. But it was still early and the children had not yet eaten, so I couldn't wait for the dance, and I said to the man, 'Dear sir, I will go as fast as I can and write it all to my dear son Hans, that he may study and pray well and be good and so come into this garden. But he has an Aunt Lena whom he will have to bring with him.' Then the man said, 'Very well, go and write it to him.'

Therefore, dear little son Hans, study and pray bravely, and tell Lippus and Jost to do so too, and you shall all come into the garden with each other. The dear God take care of you. Greet Aunty Lena and give her a kiss for me.

Your loving father,
Martin Luther

PRINCESS ELIZABETH (1533–1558)
Queen Elizabeth I (1558–1603)

This letter was written to Elizabeth's young brother, Edward. Before he became king they met frequently, studied together and were fond of each other. After he ascended the throne meetings were discouraged. Elizabeth sent him the portrait, reproduced opposite which is a companion piece to one of himself, and was probably the work of Guillim Scrots, who succeeded Holbein as court painter.

Even with modern spelling the letter is not easy to read but it has a stateliness that fascinates. Much of Elizabeth's education was based on the classics: she was an apt pupil of Virgil and could handle long sentences. From a fourteen-year-old to a nine-year-old it deserves attention.

May 15 (?)

Like as the rich man that daily gathereth riches to riches, and to one bag of money layeth a great sort till it come to infinite, so methinks your Majesty, not being sufficed with many benefits and gentleness showed to me afore this time, doth now increase them in asking and desiring where you may bid and command, requiring a thing not worthy the desiring for itself, but made worthy for your Highness's request. My picture, I mean, in which if the inward good mind towards your Grace might as well be declared as the outward face and countenance shall be seen, I would not have tarried the commandment but present[1] it, nor have been the last to grant but the first to offer it. For the face, I grant, I might well blush to offer, but the mind I shall never be ashamed to present. For though from the grace of the picture

---

[1] i.e. forestall

the colours may fade by time, may give by weather, may be spotted by chance; yet the other nor time with her swift wings shall overtake, nor the misty clouds with their lowerings may darken, nor chance with her slippery foot may overthrow. Of this although yet the proof could not be great because the occasion hath been but small, notwithstanding as a dog hath a day, so may I perchance have time to declare it in deeds where now I do write them in words. And further I shall most humbly beseech your Majesty that when you shall look on my picture, you will vouch-safe to think that as you have but the outward shadow of the body before you, so my inward mind wisheth that the body itself were oftener in your presence; howbeit because both my so being I think could do your Majesty little pleasure, though myself great good; and again because I see as yet not the time agreeing there-unto, I shall learn to follow this saying of Horace, '*Feras non culpes quod vitari non potest.*'[1] And thus I will (troubling your Majesty I fear) end with my most humble thanks. Beseeching God long to preserve you to His Honour, to your comfort, to the Realm's profit, and to my joy. From Hatfield this 15 day of May.

Your Majesty's most humbly sister and servant
ELIZABETH

---

[1] You should bear, not complain, about what cannot be avoided

JAMES STANLEY, 7th EARL OF DERBY (1607–1651)

James Stanley, MP at eighteen, Lord Lieutenant of Wales at twenty-one, supporter of Charles I, preferred the life of a gentleman farmer to that of a courtier or politician. In 1643 he retired to family property on the Isle of Man, but in the next decade the future Charles II recalled him to become part of a Royalist insurrection. He was wounded, captured, sentenced to death and executed at Bolton in 1651. From prison he wrote to three of his nine children by Charlotte, granddaughter of William the Silent, Prince of Orange.

My dear Mall, Ned, and Billy,

I remember well how sad you were to part with me, but now I fear your sorrow will be greatly increased to be informed that you can never see me more in this world; but I charge you all to strive against too great a sorrow; you are all of you of that temper that it would do you much harm. My desires and prayers to God are that you may have a happy life. Let it be as holy a life as you can, and as little sinful as you can avoid or prevent.

I can well now give you that counsel, having in myself, at this time, so great a sense of the vanities of my life, which fill my soul with sorrow; yet I rejoice to remember that when I have blessed God with pious devotion, it has been most delightful to my soul, and must be my eternal happiness.

Love the Archdeacon; he will give you good precepts. Obey your mother with cheerfulness, and grieve her not; for she is your example, your nursery, your counsellor, your all under God. There never was, nor ever can be, a more deserving person. I am called away, and this is the last I shall write to you. The Lord my God bless and guard you from all evil: so prays your father at this time, whose sorrow is inexorable to part with Mall, Ned, and Billy.

Remember

Derby

WILLIAM PENN (1644–1718)

Quaker reformer, founder of Pennsylvania

William Penn governed the colony, devised a constitution, and planned the city of Philadelphia. There was total religious tolerance, but none for card-playing or theatre-going. Penn then returned to England to help victims of religious persecution. After that he spent another two years in Pennsylvania before sailing home finally in 1701. He married twice and fathered ten children.

... my dear children, that are the gifts and mercies of the God of your tender father, hear my counsel, and lay it up in your hearts; love it more than treasure, and follow it, and you shall be blessed here, and happy hereafter.

In the first place, remember your Creator in the days of your youth ...

Next, be obedient to your dear mother, a woman whose virtue and good name is an honour to you; for she hath been exceeded by none in her time for her plainness, integrity, industry, humanity, virtue, and good understanding – qualities not usual among women of her worldly condition and quality ...

Next: betake yourself to some honest, industrious course of life, and that not of sordid covetousness, but for example and to avoid idleness. And if you change your condition and marry, choose, with the knowledge and consent of your mother, if living, or of guardians, or those that have charge of you. Mind neither beauty nor riches, but the fear of the Lord, and a sweet and amiable disposition, such as you can love above all this world, and that may make your habitations pleasant and desirable to you ...

Next, my children, be temperate in all things; in your diet, for that is physic by prevention; it keeps, nay, it makes people healthy, and their generation sound. This is exclusive of the spiritual advantage it brings. Be also plain in your apparel; keep out that lust which reigns too much over some; let your virtues be your ornament, remembering that life is more than food, and the body than raiment. Let your furniture be simple and cheap.

Avoid pride, avarice, and luxury. Read my 'No Cross no Crown.' There is instruction. Make your conversation with the most eminent for wisdom and piety, and shun all wicked men as you hope for the blessing of God and the comfort of your father's living and dying prayers. Be sure you speak no evil of any – no, not of the meanest; much less of your superiors, as magistrates, guardians, tutors, teachers, and elders in Christ . . .

. . . And as for you, who are likely to be concerned in the government of Pennsylvania and my parts of East Jersey, especially the first, I do charge you before the Lord God and his holy angels, that you be lowly, diligent, and tender, fearing God, loving the people, and hating covetousness . . .

Finally, my children, love one another with a true, endeared love, and your dear relations on both sides . . . So, my God, that hath blessed me with his abundant mercies, both of this and the other and better life, be with you all, guide you by his counsel, bless you, and bring you to his eternal glory! that you may shine, my dear children, in the firmament of God's power with the blessed spirits of the just – that celestial family – praising and admiring him, the God and Father of it, for ever. For there is no God like unto him; the God of Abraham, of Isaac, and of Jacob, the God of the Prophets, the Apostles and Martyrs of Jesus, in whom I live forever.

So farewell to my thrice dearly beloved wife and children! – Yours, as God pleaseth, in that which no waters can quench, no time forget, nor distance wear away, but remains forever,

WILLIAM PENN

Worminghurst, fourth of the sixth month, 1682

PHILIP DORMER STANHOPE
4th EARL OF CHESTERFIELD (1694–1773)

politician, diplomat, essayist, and letter-writer

Chesterfield, who is chiefly remembered for the letters he wrote to his natural son, Philip, was famous in his day as a politician who sat in both Houses of Parliament, a diplomat and a friend of both George III and the Prince of Wales.

When Philip, whose mother was a French governess, was five, Chesterfield began to send almost daily letters to him on such subjects as Duty, Learning, Good Breeding, the Lord Mayor's Show, Women, Good Posture . . . as compensation for the disadvantage of illegitimacy. They were never intended for publication. This came about when Philip died in 1768, leaving a wife and two sons who were not known to Chesterfield. The earl paid the boys' school fees but did not provide for his daughter-in-law, who published the letters to make money.

Philip was intelligent and good-hearted, but invincibly gauche. Chesterfield's godson and heir (also Philip), later a recipient of letters, loved all the country pursuits which the earl detested. But in old age Chesterfield's good humour prevailed over all disappointments and illnesses. When asked for news of his friend, Lord Tyrawley, he replied, 'Tyrawley and I have been dead these two years, but we do not choose to have it known.'

The first of any series that becomes famous has an interest of its own, so here is the first letter that the fourth Earl of Chesterfield wrote to his son, then aged five. At the beginning he sometimes wrote the letters in French, the boy's mother tongue. We are advised to take this letter as 'mere banter' in view of Philip's extreme youth, but he was probably expected to absorb the facts before he was much older. So the vast correspondence opens on a jolly tone.

(In translation.)
1737

I am told Sir! that you are preparing to go on your travels, and that you are making a start with Holland, so I thought it my duty to wish you a good journey and favourable winds. You will have the goodness, I hope, to let me know of your arrival at the Hague, and if later on, in the course of your travels, you notice anything unusual, that you will kindly send me your comments.

Holland, where you are going, is by far the most beautiful and the richest of the Seven United Provinces which together form the Republic. The others are Gelderland, Zeeland, Friesland, Utrecht, Groningen, and Overijssel. The Seven Provinces compose what are called The States General of the United Provinces, and make up a very powerful and very large Republic.

A Republic, moreover, means a completely free government, where there is no King. The Hague, where you will go first, is the most beautiful village in the world; for it is not a town. The town of Amsterdam, supposed to be the capital of the United Provinces, is very beautiful and very rich. There are several more quite large towns in Holland, like Dordrecht, Haarlem, Leyde, Delft, Rotterdam, etc. You will see, everywhere in Holland, extreme cleanliness: even the streets are cleaner than our houses are. Holland is a great trading country, especially with China, Japan, and as well with the East Indies.

There are good times ahead of you: make the most of them, really enjoy yourself; and when you come back you will have to make up for lost time by studying harder than ever. Adieu.

The next letter, which was also originally in French, but here translated, is chosen because it makes an early allusion to an important trait in Philip's character: his lack of self-confidence. Philip has asked for something that the earl considers so trivial that he hangs upon the incident a little treatise on the need for self-esteem in this life. He nicely concludes with a compliment. The letter also shows Chesterfield's appreciation of Frenchness.

Bath
29 October 1739

Mon cher enfant,

If it is possible to be too modest, then that is what you are, and you deserve more than you ask for. An amber-knobbed cane and a pair of buckles are meagre rewards for what you do, and I shall certainly add something else. Modesty is a very good quality, and is usually the accompaniment of true worth. Nothing influences men's minds so much as modesty, just as, on the contrary, nothing shocks or repels more than presumption or effrontery. A man who always wants to impress people, who is always the hero of the story he is telling, is not liked, whereas a man who, so to speak, hides his own merit, who points out that of others, and who talks little and modestly about himself, wins over men's minds and makes himself esteemed and liked.

But there is a great difference between modesty and bashfulness. Where modesty is admirable, bashfulness is absurd. You must no more be a boor than a braggart; and you must know how to introduce yourself to people, how to talk to them, and answer them without being embarrassed or put out of countenance. The English are, generally speaking, boors; they do not have the relaxed and easy, but at the same time, polite manners of the French. Therefore observe the French and imitate the way they introduce themselves and approach people. A bourgeois or a countryman is ashamed of himself when he is introduced into society; he is embarrassed, doesn't know what to do with his hands, goes to pieces when anyone speaks to him, and replies only with embarrassment, almost stammering; whereas an educated gentleman who knows the art of living introduces himself gracefully and with assurance, addresses even strangers without embarrassment, in a completely relaxed and natural way. That is what is known as being a man of the world who knows the art of living, something very important in our dealings with people. It often happens that a man of great intelligence, but who has not mastered the social arts, is not so well received as one who is less intelligent who has the social graces.

This subject certainly deserves your attention; so think about it, and let your modesty be accompanied by a relaxed, polite self-assurance. Adieu.

I have just received your letter of the 27th, which is very well written.

❖

Philip is still only seven when his father proposes they 'return' to the subject of oratory.

Bath
1 November 1739

Dear Boy,

Let us return to oratory, or the art of speaking well; . . .

The business of oratory, as I have told you before, is to persuade people; and you easily feel, that to please people is a great step towards persuading them. You must then, consequently, be sensible how advantageous it is for a man who speaks in public, . . . to please his hearers so much as to gain their attention, which he can never do without the help of oratory.

For example, suppose you had a mind to persuade Mr Maittaire to give you a holiday, would you bluntly say to him, Give me a holiday? That would certainly not be the way to persuade him to it. But you should endeavour first to please him and gain his attention, by telling him that your experience of his goodness and indulgence encouraged you to ask a favour of him; that, if he should not think proper to grant it, at least you hoped that he would not take it ill that you asked it. Then you should tell him what it was you wanted; that it was a holiday; for which you should give your reasons; as, that you had such or such a thing to do, or such a place to go to. Then you might urge some arguments why he should not refuse you; as, that you have seldom asked that favour and that you seldom will; and that the mind may sometimes require a little rest from labour as well as the body. This you may illustrate by a simile, and say, that as the bow is the stronger for being sometimes unstrung and unbent, so the mind will be capable of more attention for being now and then easy and relaxed.

This is a little oration, fit for such a little orator as you; but, however, it will make you understand what is meant by oratory and eloquence, which is to persuade. I hope you will have that talent hereafter in greater matters.

Lord Chesterfield gives advice on how to write good letters.

London
27 September O.S.
1748

. . . Your letters, except when up on a given subject, are exceedingly laconic, and neither answer my desires nor the purpose of letters; which should be familiar conversations, between absent friends. As I desire to live with you upon the footing of an intimate friend, and not of a parent, I could wish that your letters gave me more particular accounts of yourself, and of your lesser transactions. When you write to me, suppose yourself conversing freely with me, by the fireside. In that case you would naturally mention the incidents of the day; as where you had been; whom you had seen, what you thought of them, etc. Do this in your letters: acquaint me with your studies, sometimes with your diversions; tell me of any new persons and characters that you meet with in company, and add your own observations upon them; in short, let me see more of You in your letters . . . Tell me what books you are now reading, either by way of study or amusement; how you pass your evenings when at home, and where you pass them when abroad. I know that you go sometimes to Madame Valentin's assembly; what do you do there? Do you play, or sup? or is it only *la belle conversation*?

His son's letters to the earl have not survived.

Illustration from the 1798 edition
of the Works of Laurence Sterne.
The author with his wife
and daughter Lydia.

LAURENCE STERNE (1713–1768)

country parson, author

Laurence Sterne was a Yorkshire village parson. In 1741 he married Elizabeth Lumley, appreciating both her intelligence and her income. She bore him seven children, all stillborn except for one daughter, Lydia. Sterne was unfaithful to Elizabeth but suffered remorse when she had fits of insanity. When Lydia was also ill, to cheer himself up, he began on his vast satirical novel, *Tristram Shandy*. It became an instant bestseller and his life thereafter swung between bouts of dissipated jollity in London and periods of domesticity in Yorkshire.

In 1762 he travelled to France with his wife and daughter. Elizabeth elected to stay there with Lydia; Sterne eventually returned home to continue writing and to enjoy friends and flirtations in London. He loved Lydia deeply and frequently wrote to her when she was living in France.

Paris, May 15, 1764

MY DEAR LYDIA,

By this time I suppose your mother and self are fixed at Montauban, and I therefore direct to your banker, to be delivered to you. – I acquiesced in your staying in France – likewise it was your mother's wish – but I must tell you both (that unless your health had not been a plea made use of) I should have wished you both to return with me. – I have sent you the Spectators, and other books, particularly Metastasio; but I beg my girl to read the former, and only make the latter her amusement. – I hope you have not forgot my last request, to make no friendships with the French women – not that I think ill of them, but sometimes women of the best principles are the most insinuating – nay I am so jealous of you, that I should be miserable were I to ſee you had the leaſt grain of coquetry in your compoſition. – You have enough to do – for I have alſo ſent you a guitar – and as you have no genius for drawing (tho' you never could be made to believe it), pray waſte not your time about it – Remember to write to me as to a friend – in ſhort, whatever comes into your little head, and then it will be natural. – If your mother's rheumatiſm continues, and ſhe chooſes to go to Bagnieres, tell her not to be ſtopped for want of money, for my purſe ſhall be as open as my heart. I have preached at the Ambaſſador's chapel – Hezekiah – (an odd ſubject your mother will ſay). There was a concourſe of all nations, and religions too. I ſhall leave Paris in a few days – I am lodged in the ſame hotel with Mr T–; they are good and generous ſouls – Tell your mother that I hope ſhe will write to me, and that when ſhe does ſo, I may alſo receive a letter from my Lydia.

Kiſs your mother from me, and believe me

Your affectionate

L. STERNE

DR CHARLES BURNEY (1726–1814)

musician, teacher, writer on music

Dr Charles Burney was about twenty and studying music under Dr Arne in London when he met Fulke Greville. Greville, liking him and appreciating his musical ability, invited the young man to live with him. The arrangement did not last long (Greville married, then Burney), but it had great influence on Burney's life by introducing him into society and establishing him as a fashionable music teacher. He was extremely active teaching, composing, performing and writing, until a severe illness obliged him to leave London. He took the post of organist at Lyme Regis, and began to plan his *History of Music*, which is still a work of reference. In 1760 he returned to London where his happiness and good fortune were suddenly interrupted by the death of his much-loved wife.

Shortly after, he decided to find a school in Paris for two of his daughters, Esther and Susanna (Hetty and Sukey), aged fifteen and nine. Not Fanny: she is too fond of her French grandmother, and her father thinks she might become a Roman Catholic. (In fact she was to be the novelist, Fanny Burney, and she did marry a French army officer.) He writes to her with all the news.

Paris

13 June 1764

I write to my dear Fanny again, to tell her, to tell her Grandmama's, to tell her aunts, to tell her uncles to tell her Cozens, to tell all Friends that we are now at Paris . . .

We did not get here till Monday Night, owing to poor Sukey's Cough wch has been frightfully bad, & made me very unhappy . . . We have a very Good

appartment at the Hotel d'Hollande . . . There is just underneath us a Lady
Clifford in this House, who very kindly sent upon hearing that we were
English to desire to see us. She is an elderly, sensible, plain Lady without
Pride or Ceremony, & very kind to your sisters desiring them to go in & out
of her Appartme[nts] as if they were their own – There lives with [he]r
Ladyship a very pretty little French you[ng] Lady whose name is Rosalie a
little younger than Sukey an excellent play-fellow for her till she & Hetty get
settled. I have not yet seen the French Lady who is to assist me in placing
them – but shall to Morrow or next Day, when I have some Cloaths to
appear among French People in. I have found out my Friend Mr Strange,
with some difficulty – & have been with Sr James Macdonald not minding
Dress with my Countrymen. I have been excessively wretched about the
dear little Sufferer, Sukey, or Else this place & People w^d have afforded me
infinite amusement, but none greater than I have now in writing to my dear
Children & Friends in England, being my dear Fanny's most affectionate
Father – C. Burney

Paris

Monday 18(–20) June 1764

I am sure it will please my dear Fanny &c &c very much, to hear that
Sukey is a great deal better, tho' I were to write nothing Else. & indeed I
have but little Time to spare – She continued very ill here till Saturday . . .

Wednesday Night

I cannot send this away without telling you that Sukey is still better than
when the above was written, & likewise that I have now Hopes of placing
Hetty & her much to my Satisfaction. Indeed it will cost a good deal more
money than I expected, but I am now too far advanced to retreat, . . . To
Morrow is a great Festival here, when all the Streets and Churches will be
hung with Tapestry – & the finest Pictures in the King's Collections will be
exposed. There will be likewise Processions of the Clergy in all parts of the
City. Hetty & Susy have been out but very little yet, not having had proper
Cloaths: & indeed if they had been ever so much dressed Sukey was unable
to stir at Home or Abroad. I was on Sunday at the English Ambassador's
Chapel (Lord Hertford) & saw there a great many English People . . . L^d
Beauchamp son of the ambassador has been very civil to me & has shewed
me the House wch his Father Lord Hertford lives in & for wch his Lordship

gives £800 a year. It is called l'Hotel de Brancas, the name of a French Duke
now living, & is the finest and best fu[r]nished and fitted up I ever saw. Mr
Hume, Secretary to the Embassy is likewise very civil and Friendly to me, as
is Lady Clifford who lives in the same House & is own Sister to the
Dutchess of Norfolk. Indeed she is uncommonly kind to your Sisters, who
w[d] not know what to do about dress but for her Ladyship . . .

God bless you, my dear Fanny . . . Oh if you were to see w[hat] a beau they
have made of me here! – but [tho'I] sh[d] in my present dress, figure at a
Birthda[y i]n England, yet here, I am not near so fine as [a] Tradesman, who
have all the fine figured or la[ced] Silk Coats & Laced Ruffles – while mine
are only Plain. Adieu, adieu, I shall present Hetty with this bit of paper to
write down her dream upon, for she is now fast asleep at my Elbow.

MARIA THERESA (1717–1780)

Empress of Austria

Maria Theresa was the mother of Marie Antoinette, who was sent from Vienna to Versailles at the age of thirteen to be married to the grandson of King Louis XV and the future King Louis XVI. At the French court she took against Madame Dubarry, the king's mistress. Maliciously encouraged by Louis's daughters, Marie Antoinette refused to speak to Dubarry, who, by protocol, was forbidden to speak first. The Austrian ambassador, who understood that alliance between France and Austria was the aim of Maria Theresa's life, wrote to the empress, who duly wrote to her daughter . . .

The dread and embarrassment you show about speaking to the King, the best of fathers, about speaking to persons you are advised to! What a pother about saying 'Good day' to someone, a kindly word concerning a dress or some such trumpery. Mere whimsies, or something worse. You have allowed yourself to become enslaved to such an extent that reason and duty can no longer persuade you. I cannot keep silent about the matter any longer. After your conversation with Mercy and after all that he told you about the King's wishes and your duty, you actually dared to fail him. What reason can you give for such conduct? None whatever. It does not become you to regard the Dubarry in any other light than that of a lady who has a right of entry to the court and is admitted to the society of the King. You are His Majesty's first subject, and you owe him obedience and submission. It behoves you to set a good example, to show the courtiers and the ladies at Versailles that you are ready to do your master's will. If any baseness, any intimacy, were asked of you, neither I nor another would advise you to it; but all that is expected is that you should say an indifferent word, should look at her beseemingly – not for the lady's own sake, but for the sake of your grandfather, your master, your benefactor!

It was enough. On New Year's Day 1772 Marie Antoinette said over her shoulder to Madame Dubarry: *'Il y a bien du monde aujourd'hui à Versailles'* – 'there are quite a lot of people here today.' And with these words the Franco-Habsburg alliance was saved – whether for good or evil it is for historians to relate.

DR JOHN GREGORY (1724–1773)

professor of medicine, author

Gregory studied both medicine and philosophy, dividing his academic life between Aberdeen and Edinburgh, as professor of one or the other. After the premature death of his beautiful, intelligent and wealthy wife, Elizabeth, he wrote *A Father's Legacy to his Daughters*. It was published after his death and ran into several editions. He begins the *Legacy*, 'My dear Girls,' . . . Here are a few paragraphs of what he has to say on Conduct and Behaviour.

One of the chief beauties in a female character, is that modest <u>reserve</u>, that retiring <u>delicacy</u>, which avoids the public eye, and is disconcerted even at the gaze of admiration. I do not wish you to be insensible to applause; if you were, you must become, if not worse, at least less amiable women. But you may be dazzled by that admiration, which yet rejoices your hearts.

When a girl ceases to <u>blush</u>, she has lost the most powerful charm of beauty. That extreme sensibility which it indicates, may be a weakness and incumbrance in our sex, as I have too often felt; but in yours it is peculiarly engaging. Pedants, who think themselves philosophers, ask why a woman should blush when she is conscious of no crime? It is a sufficient answer, that Nature has made <u>you</u> to blush when you are guilty of no fault, and has forced <u>us</u> to love you because you do so. Blushing is so far from being necessarily an attendant on guilt, that it is the usual companion of innocence.

This modesty, which I think so essential in your sex, will naturally dispose you to be rather silent in company, especially in a large one. People of sense and discernment will never mistake such silence for dullness. One may take a share in conversation without uttering a syllable. The expression in the countenance shews it; and this never escapes an observing eye.

I should be glad that you had an easy <u>dignity</u> in your behaviour at public places; but not that confident ease, that unabashed countenance, which seems to set the company at defiance . . .

<u>Wit</u> is the most dangerous talent you can possess. It must be guarded with great discretion and good nature, otherwise it will create you many enemies . . .

<u>Humour</u> is a different quality. It will make your company much solicited; but be cautious in how you indulge it. It is often a great enemy to delicacy, and a still greater one to dignity of character. It may sometimes gain you applause, but will never procure you respect. Be even cautious in displaying your <u>good</u> <u>sense</u>. It will be thought you assume a superiority over the rest of the company. But if you happen to have any learning, keep it a profound secret, especially from the men, who generally look with a jealous and malignant eye on a woman of great parts and a cultivated understanding . . .

THOMAS JEFFERSON (1743–1826)

US President

Jefferson helped to draft the American Declaration of Independence, was Secretary of State under Washington and campaigned successfully for decimal currency. He became the third president of the USA in 1801, serving two terms, during which the slave trade was abolished, although research shows that he kept up to 200 slaves on his Virginia estate where he was born. In 1809 he retired to Monticello, near Charlottesville, to a house he designed, itself a landmark in American architecture. He was a devoted family man during his ten-year marriage; but only two of his six children survived infancy. One, Martha, known as Patsy, received this uncompromising timetable from him, in 1783, when she was only ten and staying with friends following her mother's death.

. . . With respect to the distribution of your time the following is what I should approve.
from 8. to 10 o'clock practise music.
from 10. to 1. dance one day and draw another
from 1. to 2. draw on the day you dance, and write a letter the next day.
from 3. to 4. read French.
from 4. to 5. exercise yourself in music.
from 5. till bedtime read English, write &c

Twenty-five years later Jefferson adopted a more genial tone when writing advice to Martha's sixteen-year-old son, Thomas Jefferson Randolph.

Washington
Nov. 24, 1808

My dear Jefferson – . . . I have just mentioned good-humour as one of the preservatives of our peace and tranquility. It is among the most effectual, and its effect is so well imitated, and aided, artificially, by politeness, that this also becomes an acquisition of first-rate value. In truth, politeness is artificial good-humour; it covers the natural want of it, and ends by rendering habitual a substitute nearly equivalent to the real virtue. It is the practice of sacrificing to those who we meet in society all the little conveniences and preferences which will gratify them, and deprive us of nothing worth a moment's consideration; it is the giving a pleasing and flattering turn to our expressions, which will conciliate others, and make them pleased with us as well as themselves. How cheap a price for the good-will of another! When this is in return for a rude thing said by another, it brings him to his senses, it mortifies and corrects him in the most salutary way, and places him at the feet of your good-nature in the eyes of the company. But in stating prudential rules for our government in society, I must not omit the important one of never entering into dispute or argument with another. I never yet saw an instance of one of two disputants convincing the other by argument. I have seen many of them getting warm, becoming rude, and shooting one another. Conviction is the effect of our own dispassionate reasoning, either in solitude, or weighing within ourselves, dispassionately, what we hear from others, standing uncommitted in argument ourselves.

It was one of the rules which, above all others, made Doctor Franklin the most amiable of men in society, never to contradict any body. If he was urged to announce an opinion, he did it rather by asking questions, as if for information, or by suggesting doubts. When I hear another express an opinion which is not mine, I say to myself, He has a right to his opinion, as I to mine; why should I question it? His error does me no injury, and shall I become a Don Quixote, to bring all men by force of argument to one opinion? If a fact be misstated, it is probable he is gratified by a belief of it, and I have no right to deprive him of the gratification. If he wants information, he will ask it, and then I will give it in measured terms; but if he still believes his own story, and shows a desire to dispute the fact with me, I hear him and say nothing. It is his affair, not mine, if he prefers error . . .

Look steadily to the pursuits which have carried you to Philadelphia, be very select in the society you attach yourself to; avoid taverns, drinkers, smokers, idlers and dissipated persons generally; for it is with such that broils and contentions arise . . . The limits of my paper warn me that it is time for me to close, with my affectionate adieu.

TH. JEFFERSON

P.S. – Present me affectionately to Mr. Ogilvie; and in doing the same to Mr. Peale, tell him I am writing with his polygraph, and shall send him mine the first moment I have leisure enough to pack it.

A polygraph was an eighteenth-century invention for producing copies of documents, and no doubt Jefferson, one of the world's most prolific letter-writers, found it invaluable.

Thomas Jefferson to Thomas Jefferson Smith, presumably named after the ex-president by a father proud to be his friend.

Thomas Jefferson to Thomas Jefferson Smith:

This letter will to you be as one from the dead, the writer will be in the grave before you can weigh its contents. Your affectionate and excellent father has requested that I would address to you something which might possibly have a favorable influence on the course of the life you have to live, and I too, as a responsible friend, feel an interest in that outcome. Only a few words will be necessary with good dispositions on your part. Adore God. Respect and cherish your parents. Love your neighbor as yourself, and your country more than yourself. Be just, be true, murmur not at the ways of Providence. So shall this life into which you have entered be the Portal to one of eternal and ineffable bliss. And if of the dead it is permitted to care for the things of this world, every action of your life will be under my regard. Farewell.

Monticello, February 21,
1825.

A decalogue of Lessons for Observation in practical life.

1. Never put off until tomorrow what you can do today.
2. Never trouble another for what you can do yourself.
3. Never spend your money before you have it.
4. Never buy what you do not want because it is cheap; it will be dear to you.
5. Pride costs us more than hunger, thirst and cold.
6. We never repent of having eaten too little.
7. Nothing is troublesome that we do willingly.
8. How much pain have cost us the events which have never happened!
9. Take things always by their smooth handle.
10. When angry, count ten, before you speak; if very angry, one hundred.

AARON BURR (1756–1836)

American lawyer and statesman

Burr was senator from 1791–1797 and was only narrowly defeated in 1800 when he contested the presidency against Thomas Jefferson, whom he served as Vice-President from 1801–1805. On the death of his wife, his eleven-year-old daughter Theodosia acted as hostess to the important people who visited the senator. She was well versed in Greek, Latin, maths, history, philosophy, political economy, French and German, music, riding, skating and dancing! Her father wrote her this charming letter when she was nine.

Westchester, 8th October, 1792

– I rose up suddenly from the sofa, and rubbing my head – 'What book shall I buy for her?' said I to myself. 'She reads so much and so rapidly that it is not easy to find proper and amusing French books for her; and yet I am so flattered with her progress in that language, that I am resolved that she shall, at all events, be gratified. Indeed, I owe it to her.' So, after walking once or twice briskly across the floor, I took my hat and sallied out, determined not to return till I had purchased something. It was not my first attempt. I went into one bookseller's shop after another. I found plenty of fairy tales and such nonsense, fit for the generality of children of nine or ten years old. 'These,' said I, 'will never do. Her understanding begins to be above such things'; but I could see nothing that I would offer with pleasure to *an intelligent, well-informed girl of nine years old.* I began to be discouraged. The hour of dining was come. 'But I will search a little longer.' I persevered. At last I found it. I found the very thing I sought. It is contained in two volumes octavo, handsomely bound, and with prints and registers. It is a work of fancy, but replete with instructions and amusement. I must present it with my own hand.

Your affectionate

A. BURR

It would be interesting to know the title of the book.

Theodosia always stood by her father. His life was to include a duel with Alexander Hamilton, who had prevented the success of his bid for the presidency, a trial for treason following an attempt to set up an independent government in Mexico, years of penury, and an attempt to get Napoleon's help in invading Florida. She herself married the governor of South Carolina, but in May 1812 her young son died, and the ship on which she sailed to New York to meet her father on his return from self-imposed exile was lost at sea in 1813.

THREE LETTERS IN THE LIFE OF EMMA, LADY HAMILTON (1765–1815)

Nelson's 'beloved Emma'

Emma, a poor blacksmith's daughter, was born on the Wirral peninsula, and baptized Amy, or Emy, Hart. When the blacksmith died, Emma was left with her grandmother, Mrs Kidd, while her mother sought work in London. In due course Emma, an exceptionally beautiful girl, joined her and met a dashing young aristocrat who installed mother and daughter in a cottage near his country seat in Sussex. Sir Harry Fetherstonhaugh made love to Emma; so did his friend, the Hon Charles Greville. At sixteen she became pregnant. She wrote anguished letters to Sir Harry but received no answer. So she wrote to Charles, who replied . . .

My dear Emily,

I do not make apologies for Sir H.'s behaviour to you & altho I advised you to deserve his esteem by your good conduct, I own I never expected better from him, it was your duty to deserve good treatment, & it gave me great concern to see you imprudent the first time you came to G: from the country, & as the same conduct was repeated when you was last in town, I began to despair of your happiness, to prove to you that I do not accuse you falsly I only mention 5 guineas, & half a guinea for coach, but my Emily, as you seem quite miserable now, I do not mean to give you uneasiness, but comfort, & tell you that I will forget your faults & bad conduct to Sir H. & to myself & will not repent my good humor, if I shall find that you have learnt by experience to value yourself & endeavor to preserve your Friends by good conduct & affection.

I will now answer your last letter. You tell me you think your Friends look cooly on you, it is therefore time to leave them, but it is necessary for you to decide some points *before* you come to Town.

You are sensible that for the three next months your situation will not admit of a giddy life if you had wished it, & would therefore be imprudent to come & hunt after new connexion, or try to regain the one you gave up as lost, after you have told me that Sir H. gave you barely money to get your friends, & has never answer'd one letter since, & neither provides for you, nor takes any notice of you; it might appear laughing at you, to advise you to make Sir H. more kind & attentive. I do not think a great deal of time should be lost, as I have never seen a woman clever enough to keep a man who was tired of her, but it is a great deal more for me to *advise you* never to see him again, & to write only to inform him of your determination. You must, however do the one or the other.

You may easily see my Dearest Emily, why it is absolutely necessary for this point to be completely settled *before* I can move one step. If you love Sir H. you should not give him up & if you continue with him, it would be ridiculous in me to take care of his girl, who is better able to maintain her, but besides this my Emily, I would not be troubled with your connexions (excepting your mother) & with Sir H. friends for the universe.

My advice then is to take a steady resolution, try whatever you please & if Sir H. will continue your friend, or if you prefer any other friend, do not be your own enemy, & at last if everything fails, if you mean to have my protection I must *first* know from you that *you are clear of every connexion*, & that *you will never take them again without my consent*. I shall then be free to dry up the tears of my lovely Emily & to give her comfort, if you do not forfeit my esteem perhaps my Emily may be happy. You know I have been so, by avoiding the vexation which so frequently arises from ingratitude & caprices, nothing but your letter & your distress could incline me to alter my system, but remember I never will give up my peace, nor continue my connexion one moment after my confidence is again betray'd.

If you should come to town free from all engagements & take my advice, you will live very retired, *till* you are brought to bed. You should part with your maid, & take another *name*, by degrees I would get you a new set of acquaintance, & by keeping your own secret, & nobody about you having it in their power to betray you, I may expect to see you respected & admired. Thus far relates to yourself, as to the child, Sir H. may be informed of circumstances which may reasonably make him doubt & it is not worth while to make it a subject of altercation, its mother shall obtain its kindness from me & it shall never want.

I enclose you some money, do not throw it away, you may send some presents when you arrive in Town, but do not be on the road without some money to *spare*, in case you should be fatigued & wish to take your time: I will send Sophy anything she wishes for, give her a good many kisses & a thousand to my dearest Emily. God bless you my dearest lovely girl, take your determination soon & let me hear from you. Once more Adieu my D. Emily.

Greville settled Emma and her mother in a house off the Edgware Road. When 'Little Emma' was born she was despatched to Mrs Kidd. Greville paid for her upkeep and education but would not have her as part of his household. Aware that Emma was deeply in love with him, he planned his own release by introducing her to his fifty-three-year-old uncle, Sir William Hamilton.

Hamilton took Emma to Naples where she became his mistress, then his wife. (Her mother, as always, was of the party.) In Naples she met Horatio Nelson and they fell in love. She became pregnant by him. Hamilton ignored the situation and moved them all back to London where Horatia was born in 1801. A ménage à trois was set up at Morden, in Surrey, where Hamilton died in 1803, with Emma and Nelson at his bedside.

In October 1805, the night before the Battle of Trafalgar, Nelson wrote this letter to Horatia:

20th October 1805

My Dearest Angel. I was made happy by your letter, and I rejoice to hear that you are so very good a girl and Lady Hamilton who must truly love you, give her a kiss for me. The Combined Fleet of the Enemy are now reported to be come out of Cadiz. Therefore I answer early, my dearest Horatia, to mark to you that you are ever in my thoughts.

Eight years later, Emma's protective mother was dead, and she herself was ravaged by debts, drink and illness. She also wrote to Horatia:

April 18th 1813

Listen to a kind, good mother, who has ever been to you affectionate, truly kind, and who has neither spared pains nor expense to make you the most amiable and most accomplish'd of your sex. Ah, Horatia! if you had grown up as I wish'd you, what a joy, what a comfort might you have been to me! for I have been constant to you, and willingly pleased for every manifestation you shew'd to learn and profitt of my lessons, and I have ever been most willing to overlook injuries. But now 'tis for myself I speak & write. Look into yourself well, correct yourself of your errors, your caprices, your nonsensical follies, for by your inattention you have forfeited all claims to my future kindness. I have weathered many a storm for your sake, but these frequent blows have kill'd me. Listen, then, from a mother who speaks from the dead! Reform your conduct, or you will be detested by all the world, & when you shall no longer have my fostering arm to sheild you, whoe betide you! you will sink to nothing Be good, be honourable, tell not falsehoods, be not capricious, follow the advice of the mother whom I shall place you in at school, for a governess must act as a mother. I grieve and lament to see the increasing strength of your turbulent passions; I weep & pray you may not be totally lost; my fervent prayers are offered up to God for you; I hope you will yet become sensible of your eternal wellfare. I shall go join your father and my blessed mother & may you on your death-bed have as little to reproach yourself as your once affectionate mother has, for I can glorify, & say I was a good child. *Can Horatia Nelson say so? I am unhappy to say you CANNOT.* No answer to this? I shall to-morrow look out for a school, for your sake & to *save you*, that you may bless the memory of an injured mother. P.S. Look on me now as gone from this world.

Emma died two years later. Horatia lived to be eighty, having been happily married with two children. She made a cult of her father but was also generous about her mother, without acknowledging the parentage:

With all Lady H's faults – and she had many – she had many fine qualities, which, had she been placed early in better hands, would have made her a very superior woman. It is but justice to say that through all her difficulties she invariably till the last few months expended on my education etc., the whole of the interest of the sum left me by Lord Nelson, and which was left entirely in her control.

Her behaviour to her mother was dutiful in the extreme. In fact, she should be appointed the patron saint of Home Carers, and be placed on a column as tall as her father's and close by his. There, undisturbed save for a biennial steeplejack come to clean, they could gaze at each other through the time and the weather, she with her mother's eyes.

Letters in the childhood of
ELIZABETH BARRETT BROWNING (1806–1861)

poet

As a poet Elizabeth Barrett Browning (EBB), known in childhood as 'Ba' or 'Baz', was a celebrity in her own lifetime. For her first forty-one years she was unknown, the eldest of twelve children born to Edward and Mary Moulton Barrett. The following letters have been selected to give an idea of Elizabeth's early life. The first is from her often tyrannical father, written when she was only three. He is twenty-four, a loving, conscientious head of family, by no means an ogre as yet, fulfilling a promise to a small child but also sending information to the grown-ups. Edward is away from home, looking for a country estate. (The men with whom he dined are relatives: 'your Sam' refers to his younger brother.)

EDWARD MOULTON BARRETT TO EBB

Ledbury
Tuesday Evening
[5 September 1809]

My Dear Puss,

I sit down to perform my promise of writing you. I will endeavour to inform you of the whole of our actions since I parted from you; I got to town safe, and Lockhead and myself dined with Sam, not your Sam, at whose Hotel I slept, the next morning we went to North End, where I prepared myself for my journey; We got that night, namely Saturday, to Woodstock, and the following to Malvern Town, which I meant to have been our headquarters, but we found our accommodations so very indifferent that we determined to remove them to Ledbury, to which place we took Hope-end in our way, and went on that Day nearly round the Estate, after being completely fagged, we set off for Ledbury to a very comfortable Inn; This Morn^g we again went to Hope-End and completed our tour of it, besides looking thro' the centre of the Estate and examining the Cottages; we shall go tomorrow to inspect the Timber &c – The more I see of the Property the more I like it and the more I think I shall have it in my power to make yourself, Brother & Sister & dear Mamma happy. There is no fruit whatever in the Garden, but should we be fortunate enough to be here next year no doubt we shall have abundance(.) I cant say when I shall have it in my power to return but hope at the expiration of a couple of Days more to be on my way back, that is happily as it may happen. I shall expect to see you well without any symptoms of that lurking Cough, and Buff as rosy as ever. My Best love to Mamma tell her, I believe I shall write her before my return also kiss the two other pusses for & Grandmamma, and love to Bell & Trep – not forgetting Junius –

My Paper adminishes (sic) me

I am, my Dear Ba

Y^r truely affectionate and happy Papa

E.M. Barrett

Tell that cut-throat Buff that I shall expect him, on my return to repeat Goosy, Goosy Gander &c as well as usual.

Edward bought Hope End where the family lived until 1832. From there EBB wrote her first letter to her paternal grandmother at the age of four. Elizabeth Moulton replied ecstatically:

ELIZABETH MOULTON TO EBB

(?Mickleham)

18 July – (1810)

This Morning post brought me a Letter very prettily written indeed for a little Girl of four Years old, so pleas'd am I, that I cou'd not let the day pass

without writing a few lines, to thank my Beloved Child for her attention &
expressions of Love, which I most sensibly feel – I am so proud of my
Letter that it shall be put in a very careful place, till my Darling pet grows
up, then I will shew it to you, & together, talk over the delight you took in
writing, & the raptures I experienced in reading your first performance –
Tell Papa & Mama to give you as many Kisses as I have bestowd on it,
which I assure Dr Ba are not a few; say to Papa it made me doubly happy,
putting me in mind of the time I receivd his first Letter, which I still have, &
will give you as a Keepsake when I come to see you – Ask Bro when I am to
have a Letter from him, I hope he is a good Boy, & attends to his Book –
He will never be a Man till he does –

Trepsack sends you many Kisses & is quite pleasd at your improvement,
Kisses also to Bro, Henrietta – let Mama know that you are to plead my
excuse, I intended this writing to her but cou'd not resist the pleasure I felt
to let you know how good I thought you – tell her she must not stand upon
ceremony, as she must always have a great deal to say about *you, Bro &*
Henrietta – tell Papa he too shall hear from me before long – at present I am
quite taken up with the Letter from my dear little Girl of four years old, &
can think, & talk, of nothing else –. *Junius says God Bless* little Miss, I always
knew she was very good, & am quite pleasd to see her write so well – I
suppose you will receive this in the Morn^g – when all the family are
assembled at Breakfast. You must go to each of them, & in a very pretty
manner present Trepsack & GrdMama best Love . . . Kiss dear Grandmama
Clarke for me & ask her if she is not delighted with a little Girl of our
acquaintance. My best affections with many Kisses attend

My dearest Ba

from yours truly attach^d

EM –

When she was eight Elizabeth wrote some lines on the subject of
virtue, which she gave to her father. He sent her a letter and a very substantial token of approval, addressing it to the Poet-Laureate of Hope
End. Later, she wrote in an essay that it was the word Poet which especially pleased her.

EDWARD MOULTON BARRETT TO EBB

(Hope End)
(*Docket:*
24 April 1814)

To the dear Child, whose offering this day has contributed so much to the
gratification of her Papa, who views in it not alone the Germs of [Geni]us
but the assurance that the Love of Virtue has taken such an ea[r]ly Root in
her mind. A Ten Shilling Note is sent for dear Ba to give pleasure to herself
in adding to the comforts of others.

EMB

Elizabeth determined to take a laureate's duties seriously and wrote an
ode, on their birthdays, to every member of the family. On 4 March
1820 her sister Henrietta received a Birthday Ode beginning

Time was when Phebus self was young
And music trembled from his tongue
And every Muse in youthful pride
Tuned the sweet lyre on blest Parnassus side –

and running to sixty-three lines of Miltonic imagery and classical allusion. She was surely expected to respond somehow – and Baz's birthday was in two days' time – but how to follow *that*! She is eleven years
and two days old. With dignity she addresses her sister.

HENRIETTA BARRETT TO EBB

(London)
March 6th 1820

My dearest Ba

Would you deign to read this little letter as a pledge of my affection to you; I should be glad if your genius would allow me a little of your pœtic taste, but as the muse turns her back upon poor me, and as I believe you know I try to do it as well as I can, perhaps you may excuse very dull prose and let me offer my humble wishes as well as I am able, that you may be the happiest of the happy! I hope on your next birthday I shall have more time, and more skill, to tell you how dear you are to Henrietta.

Earlier in 1820 'Bro' (Edward, Elizabeth's eldest brother) entered Charterhouse School in London. She wrote: 'If I ever loved any human being I love this dear Brother . . . the Partner of my pleasures of my literary toils . . .' She had shared Bro's tutor in Greek and Latin. Now she would be largely self-taught. They promised to correspond regularly. Here is part of a letter from Bro, originally in Latin. (Does this letter throw a light upon their father and perhaps upon Bro? Is there a hint of the tyrant in the one, a nervous haste to obey in the other?)

EDWARD BARRETT TO EBB (TRANSLATED FROM THE ORIGINAL LATIN)

(London)

Seventh day of October. My dearest Ba, I received two letters from you, one of which contained the orders of my most esteemed father, which prohibited me from leaving school, even to watch games, except when he came to the city, and from ever going to someone's home when my grandmother was not in town. I am really disgusted that I did not receive your letter sooner as I might have met with some danger of displeasing my father in some manner . . .

Elizabeth expected her young siblings to toe the party line. For a girl of fifteen her letter to the six-year-old Storm (so called because he was born in one) is a finely sustained piece of satire, but one hopes it didn't frighten the little boy out of his wits. 'Puppy' is Papa. Thomas Wallace was a reforming MP.

EBB TO CHARLES BARRETT

> (Hope End)
> (ca. March 1821)

My dearest Sir,

Neglect you? not for worlds! but at the same time let me tell you that I accuse you of shameful dereliction (tell Puppy to explain that long word) from your political principles! 'How is that pray Ba'? you will exclaim with your ugly little nose cocked up and your eyes on fire with indignation! Why Mr Storm I will tell you how that comes to pass! Because Sir you have not obeyed my positive commands. For this half hour I have been employed in examining the list of prisoners in the newspapers and have been reading with a penetrating eye the names of those condemned to the gallows! Of course I expected to see 'Master Charles John Barrett aged 6 years' at the head of them! But no! you were not even mentioned in the papers as being taken up for a slight riot – for a triffling row – or even for breaking my Lord Castlereaghs kitchen window! – Pray Sir what is the use of singing Wallace till you are hoarse – what is the use of professing radical principles if you do not act up to them? A sudden thought has struck me!! I really believe that you are afraid of being hanged! If you ARE, let me tell you Sir that you are unworthy of the cause! Nothing is more pleasant than that little tickling sensation about the throat caused by the friction of a rope! And then such a delightful view from the top of Newgate! I hope this consideration will have some weight with you if you are not influenced by any nobler sentiment and I trust that I shall ere long read this paragraph in the newspapers!

'This morning Master Storm Barrett a young man of repossessing appearance was launched into eternity! He was remarkable by the *air degagèe* with which he stepped his head into the noose' –

Adieu my dear Fellow

Your affect.^{te} Ba –

Mary Moulton Barrett, Elizabeth's mother, took a great interest in her children's education. She copied and preserved every one of Elizabeth's poems. In her letters to Elizabeth she often seems to be writing as a contemporary, someone who shares, on an equal footing, the same family preoccupations and responsibilities.

MARY MOULTON BARRETT TO EBB

(Hope End)

(ca. December 1821)

Here is frost enough my dearest Ba to make the water look like a mirror, tho' partly frozen over, and to dry & prepare the ground I trust for seed – 'Murad the Unlucky,'[1] (or rather the *improvident*) amused us all greatly last night! it is greatly superior in moral to the Arabian tales, & little inferior in incident, tho' it wants the splendor of their scenic decoration – Bro copied your half finished drawings of [...]s Cottage extremely well. I really think there [is] talent enough for the graphic art amongst all the junr branches of this house to turn it into no unworthy academy, if we had nothing else to do. – I rejoice to find that Bro has not forgotten his French either in accent or grammar – I cannot say so much for Geography. We looked over some Maps yesterday with a very wandering & unsteady gaze, & tho' I could not help feeling mortified, that knowledge to *my* mind is so needful, & to his own once so familiar should be so impaired, I still believe it is very readily regained, & willingly admit the Classics for the present to be all in all, satisfied that there *are* seeds sown of every-day knowledge which in due

---

[1] One of Maria Edgeworth's popular tales (1804)

time will not fail to yield their fruit – I am surprized to find that Sams Latin exercise consists merely of *Copying* from the grammar the four principal parts of the verbs, which any one may who can write, but the plan of the school rests upon this *extreme* attention to the most simple rudiments, & I have no doubt that the strength of the superstructure will prove its efficacy. I cannot however give up the progress Stormy is making in the advanced stage of exercises on the united noun adjective & verb, which he writes very correctly. Poor Arabel is in sad distress about her Canary, who sits moping with his head under his wing, & looks rough and miserable – it is not from want of food, but probably it feels the change from the constantly warm atmosphere of the school room, & there are some thoughts of making them [o]ver to the snug comforts of the Housekeep[er's] room for the present. Tonight I trust I will bring me good tidings of my beloved Ba. In the midst of a political tirade from Bro at tea time last night, Henry placed himself with his back to the fire, & with the Colossus stride, & his hands behind him, called out with all his might 'Imm for Teen'. Kisses to my best loved Ba from all & to all!

(I'm for Queen! Henry, aged 3, knows whose side he should be on.)

Two letters from Bro. Elizabeth has led him into an embarrassing situation, and his mock indignation knows no limits.

Daniel McSwiney, an Irishman, was tutor to Bro from 1817 to 1820. Elizabeth shared the lessons. Mr McSwiney left Hope End when Bro went to Charterhouse, but often visited members of the family in London. Brother Sam attended Charterhouse from 1822 to 1828.

EDWARD BARRETT ('BRO') TO EBB

(London)
June 22nd 1822

Upon my honour Miss Basy I hardly know how to express my indignation at the *atrocious, barefaced, unpresedented, impudent,* abominable &^{c}. lies that you are guilty of telling, dont think because yesterday the more urgent calls of hunger prevented me from paying you, that you will escape my clutches today, no, no, it is rather too good a joke to let you have your confounded whackers to pass with impunity. The charge is this that, you E.B.B. have been guilty of telling most *unfounded* falsehoods (alias confounded) concerning the Latin reading of Master E.M. Barrett, you said that the aforesaid youth declared he could read Latin better than any persons or person in the united states of Great Briton (sic) and Ireland, which declaration is as false as it is unfounded, he the said E.M.B.——tt swears to the contrary and in consequence of this abominable falsehood in presence of a M^r M^{c}S——y &c &c he was yesterday compelled to read aloud from the sixth book of the Æneid, and tormented most desperately. Sam has come and I am going for the first time walk, tomorrow I am to go with Sam to school. I must wish you good bye.

Ever believe me
your affectionately attached
Bro.

EDWARD BARRETT ('BRO') TO EBB

(London)
June 24th 1822

My ever dearest Ba.

I believe the fates have decreed that I should not forgive your deserts for your impudence however I can assure you that I shall not forget you at some other time yesterday just when I was in the middle of my bang up in came master Sam, and I was obliged to finish my letter in a great hurry before I had given you HALF your due. I should advise my friend as a well wisher of yours to send me no more of your impudence or else you shall repent it by Jove too late, no fates or anything else shall save you. Sam yesterday came home in triumph, looking half a head taller for he has got up another form, he asked Watky[1] he heard him the Greek alphabet & then put him up. M^r McSwiney dined with us yesterday and was shown your Greek epitaph, in the first place he says Anacreontic measure is not proper for an epitaph, it ought to be Hexameters & Pentameters, in the second place you must send down the translation of it, as he cannot make out your meaning. He also saw your lines which were sent to Colburns[2] and thinks them quite beautiful but it is not adapted to the public, as it is not so interesting to them not knowing the circumstances which attended it. I enclose Colburns note which he sent with the verses now dont be in a

---

[1] The Rev. Robert Watkinson, second master at Charterhouse.
[2] Colburns were publishers.

passion my friend Basy because all authors must meet with disappointment you know, I should advise you next time to send, a subject more interesting to the public. I could not go last night to school with Sam because Papa had forgotten to send a note to Watky to apprise him of my coming and therefore my bed could not [be] ready however Sam took one last night and I go this evening. Good bye my dearest Ba you must not expect to hear from me so often.

Ever believe me
Your affectionately attached –
Bro.

Granny desires me to say that though she has neglected to write to you there is nobody in this world she loves better. –

While the boys were attending Charterhouse, they often stayed with Grandmama at her London home in Baker Street, where she lived with her lifelong companion and friend, Mary Trepsack.

EDWARD BARRETT ('BRO') AND MARY TREPSACK TO EBB

(London)
July. 28th 1822

[In the hand of Edward Moulton-Barrett]
Though it threatens us rain, yet dear Granny is gone
To see 'old mother Simpson' & 'Good M[rs] Dun,'
Where your verses my Basy will make a commotion
Like Burdet or Hume on some Popular motion
The end of each sentence, & oft in the middle
With the sense incomplete and doubtful as riddle,
Dear Granny will sing till her cough interferes,
And respite is given to her auditors ears.
'What a wonderful child, what a pity it is
That her brother should have such a Mandarin Phiz!
What a wonderful child, of all knowledge no lack

What a contrast the brains to her leachy old back,
Her strains are well worthy the best of the Nine,
And her head how deserving a far better spine –
But look at her extracts – tis not to abuse you
Though in Latin it is 'Tempore et usu'
Greek, Latin, & Hebrew, serve her for quotation,
And in Justice, she brings them out in rotation,
To Italian & French she will only descend
In writing to Minny, or some Hereford friend,
Or to Bummy her aunt, or some mean burgage holder
Some reformer, Huntite, or 'Worthy Freeholder' –
At all languages used she turns up her nose
and declares against Pittites all placemen & Prose.
Dear wonderful child I would fain she wore bree[ches]
That her back was reformed, and abandon'd the leaches.'
In chorus all cry, 'We would fain she wore breeches
That her back was reformed & abandon'd the leaches' . . .

Despite the poor health and her isolation, Elizabeth determinedly pursues her ambition to be a poet. She dedicates a poem (probably 'Leila, A Tale') to Thomas Campbell (1777–1844) and sends it to him. In those days he was a highly esteemed poet, critic and editor.

THOMAS CAMPBELL TO EBB

> 30 Foley Place Portland Chapel
> (London)
> Aug: 28 1822

Madam

I should have answer'd your letter sooner but I have been unwell & very much occupied – It certainly would be very unhandsome on my part to refuse a dedication from a lady and from one who offers me so flattering an expression of her literary estimation – but as you ask also my opinion of the composition I will give you my opinion frankly for the very reason that your addressing me with confidence inspires me with a real kind of wish that my advice may contribute to your happiness & not to the contrary. – I would advise you to pause at least & to consult some other literary person with whom you can have more immediate discussion about the merits of the piece than with my self before you publish it – at least with your name – The voice of public criticism is hard & the poem is open to many objections – It bespeaks an amiable heart & an elegant mind – but it is the work of an inexperienced imagination & though the versification & expression are such as should make me very loth to exhort you to give up poetical composition Yet I should deceive you if I anticipated the story & main effect of the poem being likely to be popularly admired – I have marked one or two passages to which I particularly object – I object in general to its lyrical intermixtures – They are the most difficult of all gems to set in a Narrative poem & should always be of the first water. –

I should be heartily sorry if this unsparing criticism were to damp your poetical hopes & ambition – It is with no such intention that I comply with your request to give my judgement of this work – And rationally taken my opinion if it were of more weight than it is ought not to depress you – I am accustomed to applications of the kind & nine times out of ten decline them from a fear of discouraging an inexperienced author who may not have the sense to distinguish my motive for sincerity – Something in your letter gives me an idea that you are not of this injudicious order of literary consulters – I determined therefore to answer your note – And though it might look more like gallantry & good nature to encourage you to speedy publication yet in reality if I should mislead you by false hopes I should be acting a very unmanly & cruel part. – Give me leave at the same time to assure you that unless the perusal of your composition had given me a personal interest in you I should not risque that appearance of arrogance and severity which advice of this complexion is so apt to bear however kindly it may be meant – I trust you will believe you have a
sincere & respectful well wisher
in

Thos Campbell

At forty-one, complete with lady's maid and pet spaniel, Elizabeth eloped to Italy with Robert Browning, a greater but, at that time, obscure poet. At forty-five she bore him a son named, inevitably, after his father, but known as Pennini, or Pen. After fifteen years of supremely happy married life, she died in her husband's arms.

LUDWIG VAN BEETHOVEN (1770–1827)

composer

By the age of twenty, Beethoven, at the same time as pursuing his musical genius, was fiercely loyal to his family. His much-loved mother had died, his father was an alcoholic, he helped his brothers and his nephew out of financial difficulties.

Thayer's biography includes a letter to a young pianist, 'little' Emilie M. Beethoven's acquaintance with her contrasted with the usual turbulence of his life and the letter is a testimony to his integrity and sense of duty to the young and vulnerable. He writes warmly to a girl old enough to write to him knowledgeably, though too flatteringly, about music.

Teplitz
July 17, 1812

My dear good Emilie, my dear Friend!

My answer to your letter is late in coming: a mass of business and constant sickness must excuse me. That I am here for the recuperation of my health proves the truth of my excuse. Do not tear away the laurel wreaths of Handel, Haydn and Mozart; they possess them, but not I yet.

Your wallet will be preserved along with other things of undeserved respect from many people.

Keep at it, don't just practise art, but penetrate also to its inner laws; it deserves it, for only art and science raise men to the Divine. If you should want something at any time, my dear Emilie, write to me trustingly. A true artist has no pride. Unfortunately he sees that art has no limits; he senses darkly how far he is from the goal; and while he is perhaps admired by others, he mourns that he has not yet arrived to the point where his better genius shines as an example like a distant sun. I would rather come to visit you and your people than many rich persons who betray themselves with the poverty of their inner selves. If I should come sometime to H., I will come to you and your family. I know no other advantages of a man than those which cause him to be counted among better men. Where I find these, there is my home.

If you want to write to me, dear Emilie, address it directly here where I will be for 4 weeks more, or Vienna; it is all the same. Consider me as your friend and as a friend of your family.

Ludwig v. Beethoven

JANE AUSTEN (1775–1817)

novelist

Jane Austen had twenty-two nephews and nieces and was 'a delight' to them all according to one of them, Edward Austen-Leigh, who wrote of her 'sweet temper and loving heart'. She truly loved and enjoyed them; they interested her and made her laugh. And they loved her for the fantastic and amusing stories she told. They frequently stayed at Chawton Cottage, Alton, where Jane lived with her mother and sister Cassandra. They also submitted their own stories for her judgement. The first letter is written from brother Henry's address in London. Caroline was then ten years old.

> Hans Place,
> Monday nig[ht]
> Oct 30: [1815]

My dear Caroline,

I have not yet felt quite equal to taking up your Manuscript, but I think I shall soon, & I hope my detaining it so long will be no inconvenience. – It gives us great pleasure that you should be at Chawton. I am sure Cassy must be delighted to have you. – You will practise your Music of course, & I trust you for taking care of my Instrument & not letting it be ill used in any respect. – Do not allow anything to be put on it, but what is very light. – I hope you will try to make out some other tune beside the Hermit . . .

I am sorry you got wet in your ride; Now that you are become an Aunt, you are a person of some consequence & must excite great Interest whatever you do. I have always maintained the importance of Aunts as much as possible, & I am sure of your doing the same now. – believe me my dear Sister-Aunt,

> Yours affec[ly]
> J. Austen

Chawton
Wednesday March [1816]

My dear Caroline

I am very glad to have an opportunity of answering your agreeable little Letter. You seem to be quite my own Niece in your feelings towards M^{de} de Genlis. I do not think I could even now, at my sedate time of Life, read *Olimpe et Theophile* without being in a rage. It really is too bad! – Not allowing them to be happy together, when they *are* married. – Don't talk of it, pray . . .

Chawton
Sunday April 21st [1816]

My dear Caroline

I am glad to have an opportunity of writing to you again, for my last Note was written so long before it was sent, that it seemed almost good for nothing. The note to your Papa is to announce the death of that excellent woman Miss Elizth Leigh; it came here this morning enclosed in a letter to Aunt Cassandra. We all feel that we have lost a most valued old friend; but the death of a person at her advanced age, so fit to die and by her own feelings so *ready* to die, is not to be regretted . . .

Monday 15 July [1816]

My dear Caroline

I have followed your directions & find your Handwriting admirable . . . I have been very much entertained by your story of Carolina & her aged Father, it made me laugh heartily & I am particularly glad to find you so much alive upon any topic of such absurdity, as the usual description of a Heroine's father. – You have done it full justice – or if anything *be* wanting, it is the information of the venerable old Man's having married when only Twenty one and being a father at Twenty two . . .

Edward's [Caroline's brother's] visit has been a great pleasure to us. He has not lost one good quality or good Look, & is only altered in being improved by being some months older than we saw him last. He is getting very near our own age, for *we* do not grow older of course

Wednesday [1817]

... I look forward to the 4 new Chapters with pleasure. – But how can you like Frederick better than Edgar – You have some eccentric Tastes however I know, as to Heroes & Heroines. Goodbye

yrs affec^{ly}

J. Austen

Chawton
Wed^y March 26 [1817]

... I like Frederick & Caroline better than I did, but must still prefer Edgar & Julia. Julia is a warm-hearted ingenuous, natural Girl which I like her for; – but I know the word *Natural* is no recommendation to you ... How very well Edward is looking! You can have nobody in your Neighbourhood to vie with him at all, except Mr. Portal. – I have taken one ride on the Donkey & like it very much – & you must try to get me quiet, mild days, that I may be able to go out pretty constantly. – A great deal of Wind does not suit me, as I still have a tendency to Rheumatism. [In] short I am a poor Honey at present. I will be better when you can come and see us.

Jane Austen died on 18 July 1817.

JOHN KEATS (1795–1821)

poet

Keats's parents, Thomas and Frances, were an enterprising couple who ran livery stables at Moorfield, near London. They had four children, John, George, Tom – and Fanny, who was born in 1803 and died in 1889.

In 1804 Thomas was killed in an accident, in 1810 Frances died of tuberculosis. A Mr Abbey was appointed trustee for the children. He articled John to a surgeon; the boy qualified in 1816 and started work at Guy's Hospital. Meanwhile his first poems had been published. He gave up medicine and had his first book published in 1817. In that year he began to write letters to his sister Fanny, whom he loved dearly. But there was mistrust between Mr Abbey and the Keats boys over Fanny. Abbey kept her closely in his care at Walthamstow.

In 1818 John Keats went on a walking tour of Northern Ireland and Scotland with a friend but kept in touch with Fanny.

To Fanny Keats

> Thursday – Saturday
> 2–4 July 1818
> Dumfries July 2nd.

My dear Fanny

I intended to have written to you from Kirk[c]udbright the town I shall be in tomorrow – but I will write now because my Knapsack has worn my coat in the Seams, my coat has gone to the Taylors and I have but one coat to my back in these parts. I must tell you how I went to Liverpool with George and our new Sister and the Gentleman my fellow traveller through the Summer and Autumn – We had a tolerable journey to Liverpool – which I left the next morning before George was up for Lancaster – Then we set off from Lancaster on foot with our Knapsacks on, and have walked a Little

zig zag through the mountains and Lakes of Cumberland and
Westmoreland – We came from Carlisle yesterday to this place – We are
employed in going up Mountains, looking at Strange towns prying into old
ruins and eating very hearty breakfasts. Here we are full in the Midst of
broad Scotch 'How is it a wi' yoursel' – the Girls are walking about bare
footed and in the worst cottages the Smoke finds its way out of the door. I
shall come home full of news for you and for fear I should choak you by
too great a dose at once I must make you used to it by a letter or two. We
have been taken for travelling Jewellers, Razor sellers and Spectacle venders
because friend Brown wears a pair – The first place we stopped at with our
Knapsacks contained one Richard Bradshaw a notorious tippler – He stood
in the shape of a 3 and ballanced himself as well as he could saying with his
nose right in Mr Brown's face 'Do – yo-u sell Spect-ta-cles?' Mr Abbey says
we are Don Quixotes – tell him we are more generally taken for Pedlars. All
I hope is that we may not be taken for excisemen in this whiskey country –
We are generally up at about 5 walking before breakfast and we complete
our 20 Miles before dinner – Yesterday we visited Burns's Tomb and this
morning the fine Ruins of Lincluden – I had done thus far when my coat
came back fortified at all points – so as we lose no time we set forth again
through Galloway – all very pleasant and pretty with no fatigue when one is
used to it – We are in the midst of Meg Merrilies' country of whom I
suppose you have heard . . .

[Here he quotes seven stanzas of Old Meg she was a gypsy.]

If you like these sort of Ballads I will now and then scribble one for you
– if I send any to Tom I'll tell him to send them to you. I have so many
interruptions that I cannot manage to fill a Letter in one day – since I
scribbled the Song we have walked through a beautiful Country to
Kirk[c]udbright – at which place I will write you a song about myself . . .

[There follow many lines of doggerel.]

My dear Fanny I am ashamed of writing you such stuff, nor would I if it
were not for being tired after my day's walking, and ready to tumble into bed
so fatigued that when I am asleep you might sew my nose and trundle me
round the town like a Hoop without waking me – Then I get so hungry – a
Ham goes but a very little way and fowls are like Larks to me – A Batch of
Bread I make no more ado with than a sheet of parliament; and I can eat a
Bull's head as easily as I used to do Bull's eyes – I take a whole string of
Pork Sausages down as easily as Pen'orth of Lady's fingers – Oh dear I must
soon be contented with an acre or two of oaten cake a hogshead of Milk

and a Cloaths basket of Eggs morning noon and night when I get among the Highlanders – Before we see them we shall pass into Ireland and have a chat with the Paddies, and look at the Giant's Cause-way which you must have heard of – I have not time to tell you particularly for I have to send a Journal to Tom of whom you shall hear all particulars for from me when I return. Since I began this we have walked sixty miles to newton stewart at which place I put in this Letter – tonight we sleep at Glenluce – tomorrow at Portpatrick and the next day we shall cross in the passage boat to Ireland – I hope Miss Abbey has quite recovered – Present my Respects to her and to M^r and Mrs Abbey – God bless you –

Your affectionate Brother John –

Do write me a Letter directed to Inverness. Scotland –

Keats developed a throat condition on this tour which he could not shake off. He received a message that Tom was very ill, so he cut short his tour and reached home on 17 August. The next day he wrote two letters to Fanny.

To Fanny Keats.   Tuesday 18 August 1818
Address: Miss Keats | Miss Tucker's | Walthamstow
                              Hampstead August 18th

My dear Fanny,

I am afraid you will [think] *me* very negligent in not having answered your Letter – I see it is dated June 12 – I did not arrive at Inverness till the 8th of this Month so I am very much concerned at your being so disappointed so long a time. I did not intend to have returned to London so soon but have a bad sore throat from a cold I caught in the island of Mull: therefore I thought it best to get home as soon as possible and went on board the Smack from Cromarty. We had nine days passage and were landed at London Bridge yesterday. I shall have a good deal to tell you about Scotland – I would begin here but I have confounded tooth ache. Tom has not been getting better since I left London and for the last fortnight has been worse than ever – he has been getting a little better for these two or three days. I shall ask Mr Abbey to let me bring you to Hampstead. If M^r A should see this Letter tell him that he still must if he pleases forward the Post Bill to Perth as I have empowered my fellow traveller to receive it. I have a few scotch pebbles for you from the island of Icolmkill – I am afraid they are rather shabby – I did not go near the Mountain of Cairn Gorm. I do not know the Name of George's ship – the Name of the Port he has gone to is Philadelphia when[c]e he will travel to the Settlement across the Country – I will tell you all about this when I see you – The Title of my last Book is 'Endymion' you shall have one soon. I would not advise you to play on the Flageolet however I will get you one if you please. I will speak to Mr Abbey on what you say concerning school. I am sorry for your poor Canary. You shall have another volume of my first Book. My tooth Ache keeps on so I cannot write with any pleasure – all I can say now is that you[r] Letter is a very nice one without fault and that you will hear from me or see in a few days if his throat will let him,

Your affectionate Brother
John

To Fanny Keats

Tuesday 18 August 1818
Hampstead Tuesday

My dear Fanny,

I have just written to Mr Abbey to ask him to let you come and see poor Tom who has lately been much worse. He is better at present sends his Love to you and wishes much to see you – I hope he will shortly – I have not been able to come to Walthamstow on his account as well as a little Indisposition of my own. I have asked M^r A to write me – if he does not mention any thing of it to you, I will tell you what reasons he has though I do not think he will make any objection. Write me what you what [*for* want] with a Flageolet and I will get one ready for you by the time you come.

Your affectionate Brother
John –

Keats nursed Tom and gave Fanny news of her brothers. Relations with Mr Abbey remained strained, and he gives Fanny uncharacteristic advice.

To Fanny Keats.

Monday 26 Oct. 1818

Address: Miss Keats | Miss Tucker's | Walthamstow

My dear Fanny,

I called on Mr Abbey in the beginning of last Week: when he seemed averse to letting you come again from having heard that you had been to other places besides Well Walk. I do not mean to say you did wrongly in speaking of it, for there should rightly be no objection to such things: but you know with what People we are obliged in the course of Childhood to associate; whose conduct forces us into duplicity and fa[l]sehood to them. To the worst of People we should be openhearted: but it is as well things are to be prudent in making any communication to any one, that may throw an impediment in the way of any of the little pleasures you may have. I do not recommend duplicity but prudence with such people. Perhaps I am talking too deeply for you: if you do not now, you will understand what I mean in the course of a few years. I think poor Tom is a little Better: he sends his love to you. I shall call on Mr Abbey tomorrow: when I hope to settle when to see you again. Mrs Dilke has been for some time at Brighton – she is expected home in a day or two. She will be pleased I am sure with your present. I will try for permission for you to remain here all Night should Mrs D. return in time.

Your affectionate Brother
John –

Tom died on 1 December 1818.

To Fanny Keats

Thursday (4 or 11) Feb. 1819.
Wentworth Place –
Feby Thursday –

My dear Fanny,

Your Letter to me at Bedhampton hurt me very much, – What objection can the[r]e be to your receiving a Letter from me? At Bedhampton I was unwell and did not go out of the Garden Gate but twice or thrice during the fortnight I was there – since I came back I have been taking care of myself – I have been obliged to do so, and am now in hopes that by this care I shall get rid of a sore throat which has haunted me at intervals nearly a twelve-month. I had always a presentiment of not being able to succeed in persuading Mr Abbey to let you remain longer at School – I am very sorry that he will not consent. I recommend you to keep up all that you know and to learn more by yourself however little. The time will come when you will be more pleased with Life – look forward to that time and, though it may appear a trifle, be careful not to let the idle and retired Life you lead fix any awkward habit or behaviour on you – whether you sit or walk – endeavour to let it be in a seemly and if possible a graceful manner. We have been very little together: but you have not the less been with me in thought: You have no one in the world besides me who would sacrifice any thing for you – I feel myself the only Protector you have. In all your little troubles think of me with the thought that there is at least one person in England who if he could would help you out of them – I live in hopes of being able to make you happy – I should not perhaps write in this manner, if it were not for the fear of not being able to see you often, or long together. I am in hopes Mr Abbey will not object any more to your receiving a letter now and then from me. How unreasonable! I want a few more lines from you for George – there are some young Men, acquaintances of a Schoolfellow of mine, going out to Birkbeck's at the latter end of this month. I am in expectation every day of hearing from George – I begin to fear his last letters Miscarried. I shall be in town tomorrow – if you should not be in town, I shall send this little parcel by the Walthamstow coach. I think you will like Goldsmith. Write to me soon –

Your affectionate Brother

John –

Mrs Dilke has not been very well – she is gone a walk to town to day for exercise.

Keats went to Italy with his friend Joseph Severn and died there in Rome on 23 February 1821.

THE REVEREND SYDNEY SMITH (1771–1845)

clergyman

❖

The newly ordained Reverend Sydney Smith would have preferred to study law but had the good fortune to attract a patron who made him tutor and travelling companion of his son. In Edinburgh Smith became a co-founder of the celebrated *Edinburgh Review,* and thereafter gained a reputation as brilliant talker, wit, essayist and preacher. He held livings in London, Yorkshire and Somerset. In the latter county was the Bishop's Lydiard referred to in the following letter to his son Douglas, who was born in 1805 and died tragically young in 1829.

❖

Foston Rectory
Summer 1820

My dear Douglas,

Concerning this Mr.——, I would not have you put any trust in him, for he is not trustworthy; but so live with him as if one day or other he were to be your enemy. With such a character as his, this is a necessary precaution.

In the time you can give to English reading you should consider what it is most needful to have, what it is most shameful to want, – shirts and stockings, before frills and collars. Such is the history of your own country, to be studied in Hume, then in Rapin's History of England, with Tindal's Continuation. Hume takes you to the end of James the Second, Rapin and Tindal will carry you to the end of Anne. Then, Coxe's 'Life of Sir Robert Walpole,' and the 'Duke of Marlborough;' and these read with attention to dates and geography. Then, the history of the other three or four enlightened nations in Europe. For the English poets, I will let you off at present with Milton, Dryden, Pope, and Shakspeare; and remember, always in books keep the best company. Don't read a line of Ovid till you have mastered Virgil; nor a line of Thomson till you have exhausted Pope; nor of Massinger, till you are familiar with Shakspeare.

I am glad you like your box and its contents. Think of us as we think of you; and send us the most acceptable of all presents, – the information that you are improving in all particulars.

The greatest of all human mysteries are the Westminster holidays. If you can get a peep behind the curtain, pray let us know immediately the day of your coming home.

We have had about three or four ounces of rain here, that is all. I heard of your being wet through in London, and envied you very much. The whole of this parish is pulverized from long and excessive drought. Our whole property depends upon the tranquillity of the winds: if it blows before it rains, we shall all be up in the air in the shape of dust, and shall be *transparished* we know not where.

God bless you, my dear boy! I hope we shall soon meet at Lydiard.

Your affectionate father,

Sydney Smith

HECTOR BERLIOZ (1803–1869)

composer

Hector Berlioz was born near Grenoble, in the Dauphiné. His father was a doctor. Both parents were mistrustful of music as a career, and sent him to Paris to study medicine. But he was quite soon allowed to follow his own vocation. These two letters, addressed to his sister Nanci when he was about eighteen and she about fifteen, show already his passionately enthusiastic nature, his emotional fervour, and his love of descriptive music. Later he became a newspaper music critic, as well as writing books on music and an autobiography. We can already see his gift for writing and his ability to communicate enthusiasm.

Paris, 13 December 1821

. . . Short of fainting, I could not have had a greater experience when I saw Gluck's masterpiece *Iphigeneia*. Imagine first of all an orchestra of eighty musicians who perform with such perfect ensemble that one would think it was a single instrument. The opera begins. You see a vast plain (I tell you, the illusion is complete) and further still the sea. The orchestra presages a storm: black clouds slowly descend and cover the plain – the theatre is only lighted by flashes, in the most telling and truthful fashion. There is a moment of silence: no actor on the stage: the orchestra murmurs dully: you seem to hear the soughing of the wind (you know how in winter you can hear it speak!). Gradually the excitement grows, the storm bursts, and you discover Orestes and Pylades in chains, led by the barbarians of Tauris who sing a frightening chorus: 'We must have blood to atone for our crimes'. It's about the limit of what one can stand: I defy the hardest-hearted being to stay unmoved at the sight of these two wretches longing for death as their greatest hope – and when it turns out that it is Orestes' sister Iphigeneia, the priestess of Diana, who must sacrifice her brother, well, it is ghastly.

I can't describe to you even approximately the sense of horror one feels when Orestes, overwhelmed, falls down and says: 'Calm is restored to my breast'. While he sleeps, you see the shade of his mother whom he has killed, she is hovering about with other spirits brandishing infernal torches above his head. And the orchestra! It's all in the orchestra. If you could only hear how every situation is depicted in it, especially when Orestes seems calm: there is a long held note in the violins suggesting tranquillity, very piano: but below, the basses murmur like the remorse which, despite his apparent calm, throbs in the heart of the parricide.

But I forget myself. Farewell, dear sister: forgive me these digressions and be assured that your brother loves you with all his heart. Give my love to everybody at home.

Paris, 20 February 1822

. . . You may think that these affairs [dances] are very different from ours – not at all. The only difference is that instead of having sixteen people there are sixty, and the floor is so crowded that one must always be careful where to put down one's feet. Dress is uniformly white for the ladies and black for the men. The orchestra! You probably imagine it is superb. Well, it does not begin to compare with ours. Just think: two violins and flageolet. Isn't it pitiable? two violins and a flageolet, and those three wretches could only play contredanses taken from the ballets I've heard at the Opéra: you can imagine the contrast . . .

The next day we went to the Feydeau to hear Martin [a well-known baritone]: that evening they were giving *Azémia* and the *Voitures versées*. Ah! what a compensation for the violins and the flageolet! I absorbed the music. I thought of you, sister! How pleased you would have been to hear it! Perhaps you would like the Opéra less; it's too highbrow for you, while this touching, enchanting music of Dalayrac, the gaiety of Boieldieu's, the incredible *tours de force* of the women, the perfection of Martin and Ponchard . . . Yes, I would have thrown my arms around Dalayrac's neck had I been near his statue when I heard this air to which I cannot give an epithet: 'Thy love, O sweetest daughter', I felt nearly the same when I heard at the Opéra in *Stratonice* 'Pour your grief into your father's breast.' But I cannot undertake to describe such music to you.

GEORGE SAND (1804–1876)

French author and feminist

George Sand's real name was Amandine Aurore Lucie Dupin. She was the illegitimate daughter of a high-ranking army officer who died when she was very young. She was brought up by her grandmother at Nohant, in the Berry region of France, and married a baron at the age of eighteen. After nine years, having borne two children, she left him to pursue a Bohemian life as a writer in Paris. She dressed in men's clothing and took lovers, amongst them Frédéric Chopin. After nearly two decades of 'scandalous' living she retired to Nohant, which she had inherited, and made it a salon, including a miniature theatre, for her many friends. She took to writing plays, stories about country life, letters, a four-volume autobiography and books about her relationships with Chopin and Alfred de Musset.

Here she writes to her son, Maurice, aged about eight. The picture she describes is *Les Enfants d'Edouard* by Paul Delaroche.

Paris, July, 1831

You know, my little boy, that it makes me very sad when you do not write to me. I have received your three letters, but that is very few. It is only one letter a week. You used to write me two or three a week. Aren't you fond of writing letters any more? You need not shew your letters to anyone, nor write them so neatly that they become a task. If you send me blots and your drawings of old peasants I shall like it just as well . . .

There are such beautiful pictures in the Museum . . . The nicest one of all represents two children of seven and eight who are sitting together on a bed. One of them is ill and is leaning on his brother's shoulder. The other is quite well and is holding open a book of pictures to amuse his brother. It is a picture of two little English princes who were strangled in the Tower of London by wicked people.

Then there are a number of beautiful statues that you would recognise now that I have taught you some of the stories of mythology. The loveliest of all is *The Three Graces* in white marble; there is also a pretty little allegorical divinity, which I have never told you about. It is called *Candour* or *Innocence* and is represented by a child holding a shell from which a serpent is drinking. That means, that innocent people, just like children, never suspect the harm that bad people might do to them . . . The fêtes have lasted three days. I saw the king and all the troops from my window. Yesterday we had sports on the water. Sailors dressed in white with sashes and ribboned hats fought each other in pretty little boats. Of course they were only pretending to fight to make a spectacle. A great many of them fell into the Seine, but as they were all good swimmers they only laughed about it and soon got into their boats again . . .

In the evening I saw the illuminations from my bedroom window. There were four great illuminated columns round the statue of Henri IV. The towers of Notre Dame were illuminated too; it was all splendid. I could see the fireworks which were let off on the Place de la Revolution, from my balcony. It is a long way from me, but the rockets went up so high that I could see quite well and some them burst into flames of the tricolour. It was superb. Then there were camel races on the Champs de Mars. Men dressed up like Bedouins were mounted on horses and dromedaries. One of them had a fall and was killed . . . All the theatres are playing *gratis*, that means that one can go in without paying. Guns were fired, and petards hoisted, and bonfires lighted at every house-door, and in every street. That lasted two whole days. You might have thought there was a battle going on in Paris. I shall be very glad when it is all over and the town is quiet again. Write to me often and tell me what you are doing. Your letters are too short. Kiss your sister for me and always be very fond of her. Good-bye my dear little boy, think of your mother who sends you a million kisses.

WILLIAM HAZLITT (1778–1830)

essayist, critic, lecturer

Hazlitt, son of a Unitarian minister, grew up in the Shropshire village of Wem. He abandoned religious training to study painting, then met Coleridge and decided to become a writer. He entered the literary circle of Charles Lamb, gave lectures and greatly influenced Keats. Aged twenty, he married Sarah Stoddart, by whom he had one son, also William. To him he wrote *On the Conduct of Love: or, Advice to a Schoolboy* in 1822. The opening paragraphs are given in full. Then followed Hazlitt's views on bigotry and tolerance, satire, reading, dancing, good health, learning languages, drinking and gambling, intellectual snobbery and the unreliability of women from his own bitter experience . . . too long, alas, to be included in this book.

My Dear Little Fellow, You are now going to settle at school, and may consider this as your first entrance into the world. As my health is so indifferent, and I may not be with you long, I wish to leave you some advice (the best I can) for your conduct in life, both that it may be of use to you, and as something to remember me by. I may at least be able to caution you against my own errors, if nothing else.

As we went along to your new place of destination, you often repeated that 'You durst say they were a set of stupid, disagreeable people,' meaning the people at the school. You were to blame in this. It is a good old rule to hope for the best. Always, my dear, believe things to be right till you find them contrary; and even then, instead of irritating yourself against them, endeavour to put up with them as well as you can, if you cannot alter them. You said, 'You were sure you should not like the school where you were going.' This was wrong. What you meant was that you did not like to leave home. But you could not tell whether you should like the school or not, till you had given it a trial. Otherwise, your saying that you should not like it was

determining that you would not like it. Never anticipate evils; or, because
you cannot have things exactly as you wish, make them out worse than they
are, through mere spite and wilfulness.

You seemed at first to take no notice of your schoolfellows, or rather to
set yourself against them, because they were strangers to you. They know as
little of you as you did of them; so that this would have been a reason for
their keeping aloof from you as well, which you would have felt as a hard-
ship. Learn never to conceive a prejudice against others, because you know
nothing of them. It is bad reasoning, and makes enemies of half the world.
Do not think ill of them, till they behave ill to you; and then strive to avoid
the faults which you see in them. This will disarm their hostility sooner than
pique or resentment or complaint.

I thought you were disposed to criticise the dress of some of the boys as
not so good as your own. Never despise any one for anything that he cannot
help – least of all, for his poverty. I would wish you to keep up appearances
yourself as a defence against the idle sneers of the world, but I would not
have you value yourself upon them. I hope you will neither be the dupe nor
victim of vulgar prejudices. Instead of saying above – 'Never despise any
one for anything that he cannot help,' – I might have said – 'Never despise
any one at all;' for contempt implies a triumph over and pleasure in the ill of
another. It means that you are glad and congratulate yourself on their
failings or misfortunes. The sense of inferiority in others, without this
indirect appeal to our self-love, is a painful feeling, and not an exulting one.

You complain since, that the boys laugh at you and do not care about you,
and that you are not treated as you were at home. My dear, that is one chief
reason for your being sent to school, to inure you betimes to the
unavoidable rubs and uncertain reception you may meet with in life. You
cannot always be with me, and perhaps it is as well that you cannot. But you
must not expect others to show the same concern about you as I should.
You have hitherto been a spoiled child, and have been used to have your
own way a good deal, both in the house and among your play-fellows, with
whom you were too fond of being a leader: but you have good-nature and
good sense, and will get the better of this in time.

Hazlitt ended his letter by recommending the 'enchanting profession'
of artist to his son, surely not the first that springs to the mind of most
parents considering their children's financial security.

EDWARD LEAR (1812–1888)

artist and writer

Edward Lear was the twentieth of twenty-one children born to a prosperous family in Highgate. When he was four his father's finances collapsed and they moved to shabbier parts. His eldest sister, Ann, looked after him. She was very kind, cheerful, with a love of the absurd, and compensated for his otherwise sad and sickly childhood, for he suffered from epilepsy.

He is, perhaps, most widely known for his 'nonsense' books which reflect his love of children and the love and laughter Ann gave to his upbringing. He was also a landscape painter and illustrated his own journals and travel books.

Fanny Jane Dolly Coombe to whom he is writing here was the daughter of close friends since childhood: he wrote early humorous verse for her and her sister.

15 July [1832]

For Miss Fanny Jane Dolly Coombe.
My dear Niece – par adoption –
I shall not apologize for my departure from established rules so far as to write to one so very juvenile as yourself, – as, – from the unusual precocity of talent which you exhibited when but 6 months old I have every reason to conclude you are by this time able to read writing: – neither shall I excuse myself for quoting a foreign tongue – since I have little doubt but that if you can master English – you are equally au fait at French: – nor shall I offer any extenuation for the bad formation of my letters – for I write by Candlelight – & in a hurry. – My letter indeed is addressed to you – solely from a staunch belief that your whole kindred – friends – connexions – &

acquaintances are dead & departed – & that you, – being the youngest – are the most likely to have survived so general a wreck – thus my epistle will prove a species of dead letter – & should by rights have been preluded by a *dead*ification. Faint hopes – however sometimes reanimate my mentals. & should the sundry folks below mentioned be still on the earth – I should thank you to convey their several messages to each, – which indeed is my principle reason for troubling you with so many skewers & pothooks. If you cannot yet speak your ideas – my love – you can squeak them you know.

Tell your Aunt Eliza – that on the evening before she left London – I was taken ill – with my old complaint in the head – so much so as to be unable to walk home – which consequently prevented me from meeting her at the Coach on the following morning. By a singular fatality – also – her tortoise died the next day. Thank my friend – your uncle Robert – for his recent letter – dated March 27th.! – Tell him also – that when I ask for beasts or birds – it is only because I feel more pleasure in drawing from those given me by my intimate friends – than I could do from those otherwise come by – not from my being unable to get at specimens. – Having a rather Zoological connexion – & being about to publish British Quadrupeds – I have now living – 2 Hedgehogs, all the sorts of mice – weasels – Bats & c – & every beast requisite except a Pine Marten, – all of which, my dear child – I should be glad to present you with – did I suppose you could make the slightest use of them whatever.

Present my profound respects – to W. Wardroper Esquire – with my best thanks for his friendly communications. I am glad that his Pamphlet – 'on curing Dropsy in Gallinaceous animals,' – has so extensive a sale. Pray – my dear – tell the 2 above mentioned friends never to incommode themselves in the least about writing to me, as they are aware how obtuse my feelings are, & that I bear being forgotten with much nonchalance.

Congratulate with Mrs. Street for me, – on her recovery from her fall into the mill-pond – & from the 18 Paralytic strokes with which she was subsequently attacked: – my sister Ann is much gratified with her frequent correspondence in spite of her infirmities. – Should you see John Sayres – beg as a favour that he will not so continually torment me with graphic attention.

Tell your papa – that I have been to the Opera & have heard Paganini – both of which pleasures have greatly contributed to widen the crack which nature had originally made in my brain.

Give my kindest regards & best respects to your Grandpapa and

Grandmamma – Father & Mother – Uncle George – and Aunt Eliza – who
are not correspondents of mine – ask any body to kiss you for me – &
believe me – my dear Dolly –

Your 3 parts crazy – & wholly affectionate

Uncle Edward

61. Albany St. Regents Park – July 15.

QUEEN VICTORIA (1819–1901)

and a few of her relations

ADELAIDE, DUCHESS OF CLARENCE (1792–1849), LATER QUEEN

Adelaide of Saxe-Meiningen was married to the Duke of Clarence, who became William IV. None of William's children by the actress Mrs Jordan was legitimate, his two daughters by Adelaide died in infancy, George IV had no living descendants eligible, so Victoria became queen. Here her aunt Adelaide writes to her on her third birthday.

24th May 1822

Uncle William and Aunt Adelaide send their love to <u>dear little Victoria</u> with their best wishes on her birthday and hope that she will now become a <u>very good Girl</u>, being now <u>three years old</u>. Uncle William and Aunt Adelaide also beg little Victoria to give dear Mamma and dear Sissi [Princess Feodore, Victoria's half-sister] a kiss in their name, and to Aunt Augusta, Aunt Mary and Aunt Sophia too, and also to the <u>big Doll</u>. Uncle William and Aunt Adelaide are very sorry to be absent on that day and not see their <u>dear, dear</u> little Victoria, as they are sure she will be very good and obedient to dear Mamma on that day, and on many, many others. They also hope that dear little Victoria will not forget them and know them again when Uncle and Aunt return.

To dear little Xandrina Victoria

(Victoria's full name was Alexandrina Victoria.)

PRINCE LEOPOLD OF SAXE-COBURG (1790–1865), LATER KING OF THE
BELGIANS

Leopold was Princess Victoria's uncle. He had married George IV's
daughter Charlotte in 1816, and must have visualized a future as consort
to an English monarch. But Charlotte died in childbirth in 1820.
Leopold was not unlike Albert, who was to be Queen Victoria's consort
– a good, highly intelligent, sensitive man of liberal mind. In this first
letter, the year following his election as king of newly independent
Belgium, he writes to Victoria about his new wife, Princess Louise
Marie, daughter of Louis-Philippe of France.

Laeken
31st August 1832

My dearest Love, –
You told me you wished to have a description of your new Aunt. I
therefore shall both mentally and physically describe her to you.
She is extremely gentle and amiable, her actions are always guided by
principles. She is at all times ready and disposed to sacrifice her comfort and
inclinations to see others happy. She values goodness, merit, and virtue
much more than beauty, riches, and amusements. With all this she is highly
informed and very clever; she speaks and writes English, German and
Italian; she speaks English very well indeed. In short, my dear Love, you see
that I may well recommend her as an example for all young ladies, being
Princesses or not.
Now to her appearance. She is about Feodore's height, her hair very fair,
light blue eyes, of a very gentle, intelligent and kind expression. A Bourbon
nose and small mouth. The figure is much like Feodore's but rather less
stout. She rides very well, which she proved to my great alarm the other day,
by keeping her seat though a horse of mine ran away with her full speed for
least half a mile. What she does particularly well is dancing. Music
unfortunately she is not very fond of, though she plays on the harp; I believe
there is some idleness in the case. There exists already great confidence and
affection between us; she is desirous of doing everything that can contribute
to my happiness, and I study whatever can make her happy and contented.

You will see by these descriptions that though my good little wife is not the tallest Queen, she is a very great prize which I highly value and cherish . . .
LEOPOLD

In this letter, Leopold recommends history as a proper study for princes. Victoria is now fifteen.

Laeken
18th October 1834

My dearest Love, – I am happy to learn that Tunbridge Wells has done you good. Health is the first and most important gift of providence; without it we are poor, miserable creatures, though the whole earth were our property; therefore I trust that you will take great care of your own. I feel convinced that air and exercise are most useful for you. In your leisure moments I hope that you study a little; history is what I think the most important study for you. It will be difficult for you to learn human-kind's ways and manners otherwise than from that important source of knowledge. Your position will more or less render practical knowledge extremely difficult for you, till you get old, and still if you do not prepare yourself for your position, you may become the victim of wicked and designing people particularly at a period when party spirit runs so high. Our times resemble most those of the Protestant reformation; then people were moved by religious opinions, as they now undoubtedly are by political passions. Unfortunately history is rarely written by those who really were the chief movers of events, nor free from a party colouring; this is particularly the case in the works about English history. In that respect France is much richer, because there we have authenticated memoirs of some of the most important men, and of others who really saw what passed and wrote it down at the time. Political feelings, besides, rarely created *permanent* parties like those in England, with the exception, perhaps, of the great distinctions of Catholics and Protestants. What I most should recommend is the period before the accession of Henry IV of France to the throne, then the events after his death till the end of the minority of Louis XIV; after that period, though interesting, matters have a character which is more personal and therefore less applicable to the present times. Still, even that period may be studied with some profit to get knowledge of mankind. *Intrigues* and *favouritism* were the chief features of that period, and Madame de Maintenon's immense influence was very nearly the cause of the destruction of France. What I very particularly recommend to you is to study in the Memoirs of the great and good Sully [Minister of Finance] in the last years of the reign of HenryIV of France, and the events which followed his assassination. If you have not got the work, I will forward it to you from hence, or give you the edition which I must have at Claremont.

As my paper draws to a close, I shall finish also by giving you my best blessings, and remain forever, my dearest Love, your faithfully attached Friend and Uncle,

LEOPOLD R

Here follows a short selection of letters between some of the children of Victoria and Albert.

PRINCE ALFRED (1844–1900), FOURTH CHILD AND SECOND SON OF PRINCE ALBERT AND QUEEN VICTORIA

Alfred shared lessons with his elder brother, 'Bertie' (later Edward VII), until it became clear that the latter was exerting a bad influence over him. This is a Christmas letter to his sister, Louise, aged eight.

Geneva

22 December 1856

Dearest Louise, I wish you a very happy Christmas and I hope you will like all your prents and also my little pesant. I shall have a Christmas tree also and I will send every one of you a little thing from it I am going to have it some thing like a lottery; there will be numbers put on every little thing and then the same numbers are written on pieces of paper and then put in a bag then everyboddy pulls out one paper and see what his number is then he cuts off the little thing which has a lable corresponding with his paper.

I remain your affect. brother Alfred.

PRINCESS LOUISE (1848–1939), SIXTH CHILD AND FOURTH DAUGHTER

The queen was not fond of her but 'Bertie' encouraged Louise's artistic inclinations. She sculpted the statue of Victoria in Kensington Gardens. At thirteen, she is writing to brother Arthur, eleven.

Balmoral
13 October 1861

My dearest Arthur, I miss you so much; I am so glad that you arrived safely in London.

I have bought you a beautiful squirting ball I hope you will like it. We took our general Sunday walk by the Dee, and we were nearly blown into it. Leopold [her youngest brother, eight] and I are going to play with your fair. Mr. Leitch [their drawing master] says that he misses you very much. I am going to paint you some pictures for your book and I will give you them at Windsor. Baby [Princess Beatrice, five] speaks nearly all the day of you. I will soon write to you again and a longer letter too.

PRINCE LEOPOLD (1853–1884), EIGHTH CHILD AND FOURTH SON

Leopold, a haemophiliac, was probably the child to lose most by the early death of Albert. His father knew how to keep his mind occupied when he was obliged to lie down for long periods. He is writing to sister Louise.

Cannes
20 December 1861

Dearest Louise,

I was so very very much grieved when I heard of the death of poor dear Papa, who I loved so very very much, I got a letter from you this morning in which you said a great deal of the death of poor dear Papa, it is such a fearful loss I am so very much grieved. Dear Louise please to not forget to send me the studs . . . for Dr. Günther as a Christmas present . . . I hope Mama is quite well.

The queen, of course, was not 'quite well'. She had embarked upon years and years of deep mourning.

ALBERT EDWARD, PRINCE OF WALES (1841–1901), KING (1901–1910)

He is here thanking his sister Louise, fifteen, for a twenty-second birthday present.

Sandringham
10 November 1863

The little statuette is really admirably modelled, and I strongly advise you to continue taking lessons with Mrs. Thornycroft as you certainly have great talent in modelling, and may perhaps become some day an eminent sculptress.

PRINCESS LOUISE TO PRINCE ARTHUR (THIRTEEN)

Lenchen is Helen, the tomboy of the family, then sixteen.

3 February 1863

. . . Mama gave a council this morning and the Archbishop of York did homage, Lenchen was present, she said that Mama held his hands up whilst he was taking [the] oath and then afterwards he kissed the Bible. Lenchen said she felt such an inclination to laugh.

QUEEN VICTORIA (1819–1901)

Here Queen Victoria writes to her granddaughter Victoria, whose mother, Princess Alice, had died after nursing her entire family through diphtheria. The queen writes on the first anniversary of Alice's death.

WINDSOR CASTLE
Dec 12 1879

Darling Victoria,

I write these lines to arrive on that *dreadful* day wh took your darling Mama as well as 17 years before your darling Grandpapa away from their happy homes. Unfortunately you had not, as dear Mama had had, the blessing & privilege of being with her during her illness & at the *last*, when she passed away, as she had of being with her beloved Parent to the last moment & of seeing him while ill. And I as near my *own* beloved Mother when she died. *This* I grieve for your sake was denied to you – as you were not able to have that blessed & sacred recollection of it for life! But as life goes on and you get older, & require the support & advice of a loving

Mother you will more & more feel the terrible loss! Let *every* day bring you nearer to her & to her dear memory. Think how she gave her life out of love for you all!

Be all you can to poor Papa & your brother & sisters. So much depends on you darling Victoria as the eldest.

We shall all go to the Mausoleum for a short service there at 11.30 on the morning of the sad 14th and in the aft'noon at evg. Service in the Chapel here. Mr. T. Shore will preach.

God bless you darling child, you know you can always look on me as a Mother.

Ever your devoted Grandmama

V.R.I.

T.O. How every day <u>now</u> reminds me of this terrible last year – living between hope & fear! Speak to the others <u>from me</u>!

FELIX MENDELSSOHN (1809–1847)

composer

Felix Mendelssohn was founder-director of the Leipzig Conservatory where Ignaz Moscheles (1794–1870) was his friend and highly appreciated head of the piano department. When he heard of the birth of Moscheles's son, he sent his colleague a highly unusual gift for the little boy, with a commentary.

Mendelssohn, for his godson

'So he is to be called Felix, is he? How nice and kind of you to make him my godchild in forma! The first present his godfather makes him is the above entire orchestra; it is to accompany him through life, the trumpets when he wishes to become famous, the fiddles when he falls in love, the cymbals when he grows a beard; the piano explains itself; and should people ever play him false, as will happen to the best of us, there stand the kettledrums and the big drum in the background.'

EDWARD DICKINSON (c.1800?–1874)
lawyer, US Congressman

Dickinson was the father of the American poet Emily Dickinson (1830–1886). He had three children, of whom Emily's biographer wrote 'They tended to take after their strong-minded father rather than their more ineffectual mother . . .' How much of what Edward wrote in the following intimidatingly phrased letter rubbed off? Emily was only seven when she received it. She led a seemingly normal life until, in her mid-twenties, and of her own volition, she became a prisoner in the family home at Amherst, Massachusetts, avoiding meetings with all but a few people. Only seven of her poems were published in her lifetime.

Winter 1837 or 1838

. . . I want to have you do perfectly right – always be kind & pleasant, & always tell the truth, & never deceive. That is the way to become good . . . I want to have you grow up & become good men & women – and learn all you can, so that you can teach others to do right. You have enough to eat & drink, & good clothes – & go to school – while a great many poor little children have to go hungry – and have ragged clothes – & sleep cold, & have poor green wood to burn, & can't have books or go to school. All you learn, now, when you are young, will do you a great deal of good, when you are grown up . . .

AMOS BRONSON ALCOTT (1799–1888)

teacher and educationist

Amos Bronson Alcott was the father of Louisa May Alcott, author of *Little Women*. His ideas on education were unorthodox, involving a great deal more freedom than the more usual systems. They no doubt contributed to the background of *Little Men*, in which Jo and her husband, Professor Bhaer, run a home and school for boys.

Mr Alcott was a transcendental Christian. He counted among his friends Ralph Waldo Emerson (possibly the model for Professor Bhaer) and Henry Thoreau.

My Daughter,

You are seven years old to-day and your Father is forty. You have learned a great many things, since you have lived in a Body, about things going on around you and within you. You know how to think, how to resolve, how to love, and how to obey. You feel your Conscience, and have no real pleasure unless you obey it. You cannot love yourself, or anyone else, when you do not mind its commandments. It asks you always to BE GOOD, and bears, O how gently! how patiently! with all endeavors to hate, and treat it cruelly. How kindly it bears with you all the while. How sweetly it whispers Happiness in your HEART when you Obey its soft words. How it smiles upon you, and makes you Glad when you Resolve to Obey it! How terrible its PUNISHMENTS. It is GOD trying in your soul to keep you always Good.

You begin, my dear daughter, another year this morning. Your Father, your Mother, and Sisters, with your little friends, show their love on this your Birthday, by giving you this BOX: Open it, and take what is in it; and the best wishes of

Your Father.

Beach Street,
Friday Morning, Nov. 29, 1839

ABBA MAY ALCOTT (1800–1877)

She was the mother of the author Louise May Alcott. Here are two birthday letters to Louisa, in which anyone familiar with the books will recognize first Marmee and then Jo herself in the advice to 'Go on trying, dear . . .' The third letter strangely foretells exactly what did happen.

My dear little girl,

Will you accept this doll from me on your 7th birthday. She will be a quiet play mate for my active Louisa for seven years more. Be a kind mamma and love her for my sake.

Your mother

Beach St., Boston, 1839

Cottage in Concord

Dear Daughter

Your 10th birthday has arrived, may it be a happy one, & on each returning birthday may you feel new strength and resolution to be gentle with sisters, obedient to parents, loving to everyone & happy in yourself.

I give you the pencil case I promised, for I have observed that you are fond of writing, and wish to encourage the habit.

Go on trying dear, & each day it will be easier to be & do good. You must help yourself, for the cause of your little troubles is in yourself & patience & courage only will make you what mother prays to see you her good and happy girl.

Concord, 1843

Dear Louy,

I enclose a picture for you which I always liked very much, for I have imagined that you might be just such an industrious daughter & I such a feeble but loving mother, looking to your labor for my daily bread. Keep it for my sake, & your own, for you and I always liked to be grouped together.

Mother

VICTOR HUGO (1802–1885)

French novelist, poet and dramatist

Hugo, a leading member of the Romantic movement, was born into a military family at Besançon. His first poems appeared when he was only twenty. He wrote prolifically all his life, Verdi adapted two of his verse plays for operas, his novel, *Les Misérables*, has become a hit musical, and another, *Notre Dame de Paris*, has been filmed several times He was made a senator out of recognition for his lifelong work as a libertarian. His daughter Adèle – Dédé – was born in 1830: she seems to be the one member of the family who writes to him.

1839

Ma Dédé, ma chère petite Dédé

I love you. Your dear little letter gave me great pleasure and I am going to try and write so that you can read this one yourself. When you receive it you will be just about to leave for Paris, where you will no longer have those delightful twins or the parks, where you will no longer see pictures by Raphael, but you will soon see your petit papa who loves you so much.

I too, I shall be leaving a beautiful sea covered with beautiful boats, but I shall be seeing my dear little Dédé.

Dear child, put a kiss for me on the two eyes of your good mother, tell her that I love her very much and tell her to write to me. And you, write to me at Chalons-sur-Saone. Another kiss, my beloved Dédé

Ton petit papa.

1840

I must also thank you, ma Dédé, mon pauvre amour. You have written me yet another charming little letter that you have dated for which I am very touched because there is only you in the whole family who dreams of dating letters. So there you are back in Paris.

Dear child, you have bravely left behind you all the pleasures of Villequiers and you have got down to work again like the good little girl that you are. So your daddy loves you. See you soon my angel. Kiss your mother for me as you have already done before, and Charlot as well and Toto also. In a few days I will give you back all the kisses that you have spent.

Ton petit papa

1843

Do you know, ma Dédé, that you have written me a charming letter? You must write to me like that very often. I will answer as often as I can. Your mother and Didine are a couple of lazybones. Scold them because they haven't written to me, and then kiss them because I love them . . .

Have you scolded your happy and pretty sister who laughs all the time? Have you told her to write to me? Did you scold her really hard?

1843

I haven't been able to find the books that you asked me for. You see, my dear little girl that you must be methodical when you go away and be careful to take away everything that you will need. One moment's forgetfulness can bring a month of inconvenience and waiting about and wasted time.

However, you must work, mon cher bijou, I ask it of you just as much as of Toto. I also recommend it to both of you to enjoy yourselves and keep well.

CHARLES DODGSON (1800–1868)

cleric

Charles Dodgson, the father of Lewis Carroll, was, at the time of writing this letter, Perpetual Curate of Daresbury, Cheshire. He later became Archdeacon of Richmond, Yorkshire. He married Frances Jane Lutwidge, daughter of an army officer. Church and army predominate in the ancestry of 'Lewis Carroll'. When this letter was written Charles the son was eight years old.

Ripon
January 6, 1840

My dearest Charles,

I am very sorry that I had not time to answer your nice little note before. You cannot think how pleased I was to receive something in your handwriting, and you may depend upon it I will not forget your commission. As soon as I get to Leeds I shall scream out in the middle of the street, *Ironmongers, Ironmongers*. Six hundred men will rush out of their shops in a moment – fly, fly, in all directions – ring the bells, call the constables, set the Town on fire. I will have a file and a screwdriver and a ring and if they are not brought directly in forty seconds, I will leave nothing but one small cat alive in the whole Town of Leeds, and I shall only leave that, because I am afraid I shall not have time to kill it. Then what a bawling and a tearing of hair there will be! Pigs and babies, camels and butterflies, rolling in the gutter together – old women rushing up the chimneys and cows after them – ducks hiding themselves in coffee-cups, and fat geese trying to squeeze themselves into pencil cases. At last the Mayor of Leeds will be found in a soup plate covered up with custard, and stuck full of almonds to make him look like a sponge cake that he may escape the dreadful destruction of the

Town. Oh! where is his wife? She is safe in her own pincushion with a bit of sticking plaster on the top to hide the hump in her back, and all her dear little children, seventy-eight poor little helpless infants crammed into her mouth, and hiding themselves behind her double teeth. Then comes a man hid in a teapot crying and roaring, 'Oh, I have dropped my donkey. I put it up my nostril, and it has fallen out of the spout of the teapot into an old woman's thimble and she will squeeze it to death when she puts her thimble on.'

At last they bring the things which I ordered, and then I spare the Town, and send off in fifty waggons, and under the protection of ten thousand soldiers, a file and a screwdriver and a ring as a present to Charles Lutwidge Dodgson, from

his affectionate Papa

MRS ELIZABETH CLEGHORN GASKELL
(1810–1865)

author

Mrs Gaskell, as she is always called, was born Elizabeth Cleghorn Stevenson, daughter of a Unitarian minister. Her mother having died, she was adopted, aged one, by an aunt and brought up at Knutsford, Cheshire (the model for Cranford in her most famous novel). At twenty-two she married a Unitarian minister by whom she had six children. The only boy, William, died aged ten months. To combat her grief, Mrs Gaskell wrote *Mary Barton*, an innovative novel in that all its characters are working class. It was an instant success despite vociferous criticism.

When her eldest surviving daughter Marianne (Polly) was fifteen, the girl was sent to study music in Hampstead. Mrs Gaskell wrote to her frequently in letters that had no truck with the paragraph.

Monday, morning
Plymouth Grove
[Manchester
17 February 1851]

My dearest Polly,
Papa is gone to breakfast with the High Sheriff, about which we have been laughing a great deal at him, and telling him he would be expected in a helmet and white cravat; as he and some other gentlemen are to take the High Sheriff (Mr. Percival Heywood) to meet the judge. Flossy and Meta are going with Mrs. Shuttleworth to see the show at 11, so that is the state of commotion our house is in. I was sorry that I could not write, as I intended yesterday; but Emily Winkworth came to spend the afternoon and evening.

She is now staying in Dundas Place. I must try and tell you things a little more in order. I don't know how it is, but we all seem to have got into our heads that *we* might only write *once* a week to *you*; which is a mistake is it not? but owing to it you had no letter last week, which shan't occur again, dear. Your yesterday's letter was a charming one; full of detail, and very satisfactory. I fancy this plan of only writing once a week is a very good one for you; it makes you think of all you want to say, and not write such good-for-nothing hurried letters as you used to do. Pray take pains about Pergetti. I have promised Papa such nice singing at Midsummer. I don't mean only take pains when he is there; but remember all his advice &c when you are practising; for you must either practise well or ill; and practising ill & carelessly only *confirms* you in *bad* habits. You ought to try and imagine the expression with which songs ought to be sung, according to their *words*, and meaning, and not be dependent upon pencil marks and accents; which is a very mechanical way of getting expression. The accident we had in coming down was simply this, the pilot-engine (sent before to clear the way for an express train) got broken, and stopped the *down*-line; so we had to wait 2 hours and a half in a very dull place, not at a station, and with a great white chalk bank on either side, waiting till all the *up*-trains had gone by that we might go back to the last station and go on the *up*-line without fear of an accident; it was only dull not dangerous.

Monday
[7 April 1851]

My dearest Polly,

I have no paper but this and too bad a cold to go out; so I shall write as far as it will go; and wait for the remainder. Pray *why* do you wish a Protectionist Ministry not to come in? Papa and I want terribly to know. Before you fully make up your mind, read a paper in the Quarterly on the subject of Free Trade (written by Mr. George Taylor) in (I think) the year 1839; and then when you come home I will read with you Mr. Cobden's speeches [.] But first I think we should read together Adam Smith on the Wealth of Nations. Not confining ourselves as we read to the limited meaning which he affixes to the word 'wealth'. Seriously, dear, you must not become a *partizan* in politics or in anything else, – you must have a 'reason for the faith that is in you', – and not in three weeks suppose you can know enough to form an opinion about measures of state. That is one reason why so many people dislike that women should meddle with politics; they say it is a subject requiring long patient study of many branches of science; and a logical training which few women have had, – that women are apt to take up a thing without being even able to state their reasons clearly, and yet on that insufficient knowledge they take a more violent and bigoted stand than thoughtful *men* dare to do. Have as many and as large and varied interests as you can; but do not again give a decided opinion on a subject on which you can at present know nothing. About yr bonnet get it *large*, and trimmed with (– or) white [.] ARE your shoulders lower? If not, and dancing or exercises will bring them down have another quarter & welcome. Papa will send you compasses by somebody and perhaps Shakspeare. Be sure you take care of MY *cameo* brooch. I find you have got it; now I only lent it to you and I value it extremely, and would not have it lost on any account.

LEWIS CARROLL (1832–1898)

writer, academic, cleric

Lewis Carroll was born Charles Lutwidge Dodgson. The creator of *Alice in Wonderland* came from a family with church and army antecedents (see p. 87) and a deep appreciation of literature and art. He became an inventor of ciphers and educational board games, wrote books on mathematics and many letters to children, including among them Alice Liddell, who inspired his most famous works. Alice's mother burned them all and the corresponding period of his diary has been cut out. We do not know why.

The first letter is to his young sister (twelve) and brother (nine).

[Christ Church, Oxford]
January 31, (1855?)

My dear Henrietta
My dear Edwin,

I am very much obliged by your nice little birthday gift – it was much better than a cane would have been – I have got it on my watch chain, but the Dean has not yet remarked it.

My one pupil has begun his work with me, and I will give you a description how the lecture is conducted. It is the most important point, you know, that the tutor should be *dignified*, and at a distance from the pupil, and that the pupil should be as much as possible *degraded* – otherwise you know, they are not humble enough. So I sit at the further end of the room; outside the door (*which is shut*) sits the scout outside the outer door (*also shut*) sits the sub-scout; half-way down stairs sits the sub-sub-scout; and down in the yard sits the *pupil*.

The questions are shouted from one to the other, and the answers come back in the same way – it is rather confusing till you are well used to it. The lecture goes something like this.

Tutor. 'What is twice three?'

Scout. 'What's a rice tree?'

Sub-Scout. 'When is ice free?'

Sub-sub-Scout. 'What's a nice fee?'

Pupil (timidly). 'Half a guinea!'

Sub-sub-Scout. 'Can't forge any.'

Sub-Scout. 'Ho for Jinny!'

Scout. 'Don't be a ninny!'

Tutor (looks offended, but tries another question). 'Divide a hundred by twelve!'

Scout. 'Provide wonderful bells!'

Sub-Scout. 'Go ride under it yourself.'

Sub-sub-Scout. 'Deride the dunder-headed elf!'

Pupil (surprised). 'What do you mean?'

Sub-sub Scout. 'Doings between!'

Sub-Scout. 'Blue is the screen!'

Scout. 'Soup-tureen!'

And so the lecture proceeds.

Such is Life – from

Your most affectionate brother,

Charles L. Dodgson

TO MARY MACDONALD

Mary, then aged about eleven, was the daughter of the writer George MacDonald; she had a brother, Greville. Carroll read *Alice* to them in manuscript at Mrs MacDonald's request. At the end, Greville declared he would like '60,000 volumes of it'. Later he said that what he particularly liked about Carroll's stories was that they had 'no moral hint to spoil the fun'. (Carroll had been ordained into the Church of England in 1861!)

In a few of his letters Carroll seems to be gently instructing his young correspondent in how to recognize irony, and the absurd. His afterthought seems like a neat little exercise a good teacher might set to make sure a point has been understood.

Christ Church, Oxford
May 23, 1864

My dear Child,

It's been so frightfully hot there that I've been almost too weak to hold a pen, and even if I had been able, there was no ink – it had all evaporated into a cloud of black steam, and in that state it has been floating about the room inking the walls and ceiling till they're hardly fit to be seen: today it is cooler, and a little has come back into the ink-bottle in the form of black snow – there will soon be enough for me to write and order those photographs your Mamma wants.

This hot weather makes me very sad and sulky: I can hardly keep my temper sometimes. For instance, just now the Bishop of Oxford came in to see me – it was a civil thing to do, and he meant no harm, poor man: but I was so provoked at his coming in that I threw a book at his head, which I am afraid hurt him a great deal (Mem: this isn't quite true, so you needn't believe it. Don't be in such a hurry to believe next time – I'll tell you why. If you set to work to believe everything, you will tire out the believing-muscles of your mind, and then you'll be so weak you won't be able to believe the simplest true things. Only last week a friend of mine set to work to believe Jack-the-giant-killer. He managed to do it, but he was so exhausted by it that when I told him it was raining (which was true) he *couldn't* believe it, but rushed out into the street without his hat or umbrella, the consequences of which was his hair got seriously damp, and one curl didn't recover its right shape for nearly 2 days. (Mem: some of *that* is not quite true, I'm afraid.)) Will you tell Greville I am getting on with his picture (to go into the oval frame, you know) and I hope to send it in a day or two. Also tell your Mamma that I'm sorry to say none of my sisters are coming to London this summer.

With my kind regards to Papa and Mamma, and love to you and the other infants, I remain

Your affectionate Friend
Charles L. Dodgson

The only unlucky thing that happened to me last Friday was *your* writing to me. There!

TO AGNES ARGLES

Agnes ('Dolly'), then aged ten, had been urged by her family and friends to write to Mr Charles Lutwidge Dodgson, to ask when he was going to write another book. He replied: 'I have a message for you from a friend of mine, Mr Lewis Carroll, who is a queer sort of creature, rather too fond of talking nonsense . . .' He met Dolly the following year. Later she gave him a present.

Christ Church, Oxford
(April 17?, 1868)

My dear Dolly,

You can't think how useful that present of yours was, all the way up to London! Perhaps you remarked that old lady who was sitting next me in the carriage? I mean the one with hooked eyes and a dark blue nose. Well, the moment the train went off, she said to me (by the by, it was her language that first made me think she wasn't *quite* a lady) she said to me, 'Was them three young ladies on the plank-form, what held their hankerchers to their eyes, a shedding crystal tears, or was they shamming?' I didn't like to correct her, even by speaking correctly myself, so I said, 'They *was* shedding real tears, mum, but tears ain't crystials.' She said, 'Young man, you hurts my feelings!' and she began to cry.

I tried to comfort her by saying cheerfully, 'Now don't *you* shed crystial tears. Won't a little brandy do you good?' 'No!' she said. 'No brandy – poetry, poetry!'

So I got your book out, and handed it to her, and she read it all the rest of the way, only sobbing a little now and then: when she gave it back she said, 'Tell the young lady as give it yer, which I see her name is Dolly, ??? poetry's

the thing! Let her read that, and she'll shed no more crystial tears.' And she
went off repeating, ''tis the voice of the lobster.' So I thought I would write
and give you her message.

Tell Edith I send her a key-word, if she wants to try her hand at writing in
cipher, but tell her also that I should think her parents will highly approve of
such conduct.

How is Fix* going on?

Give my love to Lily*

Some children have a most disagreeable way of getting grown-up: I hope
you won't do anything of that sort before we meet again.

With kind regards to the party, I am

Yours affectionately,

C.L. Dodgson

TO JULIA AND ETHEL ARNOLD

Julia, who became the mother of Julian and Aldous Huxley, was a
favourite among Carroll's photographic models. Ethel remembered the
magic of visiting his rooms in Oxford, where cupboards ran all round
the sitting room – an Aladdin's cave of 'mechanical beasts, dancing
dolls, toys and puzzles of every description'.

In this letter Carroll asks, in a highly original manner, for a book to
be returned.

(Christ Church, Oxford)

(March 3?, 1874)

What remarkably wicked children you are! I don't think you would find in
all history, even if you go back to the times of Nero and Heliogabalus, any
instance of children so heartless and so entirely reckless about returning
story-books. Now I think of it, neither Nero nor Heliogabalus ever failed to
return any story-book they borrowed. That is certain, because they never

---

* Two dogs belonging to the family.

borrowed any, and that again is certain because there were none printed in those days.

Affectionately yours,

C.L.D.

Carroll liked to take his child-friends to the theatre. In 1877 *Goody Two Shoes* was his choice, in which 'Little Bertie Coote (about 10) was Clown, a wonderfully clever little fellow . . .' The boy remembered how 'Mr Dodgson' often came behind the scenes. In his opinion, if Carroll had not been afflicted by a slight stutter in the presence of grown-ups, he would have made a wonderful actor. Bert wanted a letter from this marvellous and lovable man. This is it.

The Chestnuts,
Guildford
June 9 (?1877)

My dear Bertie,

I would have been very glad to write to you as you wish, only there are several objections. I think, when you have heard them, you will see that I am right in saying 'No.'

The first objection is, I've got no ink. You don't believe it? Ah, you should have seen the ink there was in *my* days! (About the time of the battle of Waterloo: I was a soldier in that battle.) Why, you only had to pour a little of it on the paper, and it went on by itself! *This* ink is so stupid, if you begin a word for it, it can't even finish it by itself.

The next objection is, I've no time. You don't believe *that*, you say? Well, who cares? You should have seen the time there was in *my* days! (At the time of the battle of Waterloo, where I led a regiment.) There were always 25 hours in the day – sometimes 30 or 40.

The third and greatest objection is, my *great* dislike for children. I don't know why, I'm sure: but I *hate* them – just as one hates arm-chairs and plum-pudding! You don't believe *that*, don't you? Did I ever say you would? Ah, you should have seen the children there were in my days! (Battle of Waterloo, where I commanded the English army. I was called 'the Duke of Wellington' then but I found it a great bother having such a long name, so I changed it to 'Mr. Dodgson.' I chose that name because it begins with the same letter as 'Duke.') So you see it would never do to write to you.

Have you any sisters? I forget. If you have, give them my love. I am much obliged to your Uncle and Aunt for letting me keep the photograph.

I hope you won't be much disappointed at not getting a letter from me.

Your affectionate friend,

C.L. Dodgson

GUSTAVE FLAUBERT (1821–1880)

novelist

When Flaubert failed his law examinations, he was unwell, so his parents allowed him to stay at home with them in Rouen and devote himself to literature. Caroline, a younger sister, completed a happy family. She married at twenty and died in childbirth the following year, 1846. In the same year Gustave's father died, so Madame Flaubert and her son, with Caroline's motherless baby daughter, moved to their country house at Le Croisset. The grandmother saw to the child's physical needs, Gustave looked after her education. She, also named Caroline, did not return or repay their affection. In the second letter to her here, Flaubert includes a pen-portrait of himself as a writer which may well have mystified her.

Flaubert to his niece Caroline, aged ten.

Paris, 25th April 1856

I haven't behaved very well towards you, my poor little soul, in not replying to the nice letter you wrote me a long time ago, I see. Accept my apologies. I have been very busy.

But that wasn't a reason for stopping our correspondence. You could easily have written to me just the same. You could have told me if you were enjoying yourself and given me news of your grandmother who hasn't been well.

Have you been looking after her properly? Have you been really kind to her?

You have to take the place of your poor mother, who was so good, so intelligent, and so beautiful. Do everything you can to make your grandmother happy and able to forget her unhappiness. Next year you will make your first communion. It's the end of childhood. You will be a young person. Think about it! It's the moment to have all the virtues.

Did the priest at Canteleu think you were good at your catechism?

How is your rabbit?

Was your straw hat a success?

Write to me next week. I still mean to come back on Saturday. And from the following Monday we'll start our lessons again. I hope your little noddle has had a good rest, and that we'll get on fast. In any case we must finish Roman history this summer.

Good-bye, my puss, give your grandma a kiss for me. And go on loving your old uncle.

To Caroline, aged eleven.

[Paris]
Friday [24 April 1857]

Ma chère Lilinne,

Thank you very much for writing me such a nice letter. The spelling is better than in those which you have sent me from previous journeys, and the style is equally good. By virtue of sitting down in my armchair, putting your elbows on my table and taking your head in both hands, perhaps you'll end up by becoming a writer.

There's a lady here whom I met in the street and who is staying in my study where she is gently laid on one of my bookshelves. Her clothes are very light, just a sheet of paper which wraps her from head to foot. The poor young lady has nothing but her hair, her shift, her stockings and shoes. She's looking forward to my departure because she knows that at Croisset she'll find clothes more appropriate for the modesty demanded by her sex.

Thank Mme Robert on my behalf. She wanted to be remembered to me. Pay her my respects and advise her to adopt a strengthening diet because she seems to me to be a little pale and I am somewhat concerned for her health.

Yesterday I went to an exhibition of paintings, and I thought a lot about you, pauvre chérie. There were many subjects that you would have recognised, thanks to your learning, and several portraits of great men that you would have known too. I even saw several pictures of rabbits. – And I searched in the catalogue to see if I could find the name *Rabbit*, the landlord at Croisset. But it wasn't there.

Tell your mother that I am going to Mme Laurent soon, and that she will get a letter from me on Sunday. I have only just received hers.

Adieu, mon pauvre loulou. Kiss your grandmother for me.

Your uncle who loves you.

Shake hands with Miss Green for me, and be polite to her if you want to please me.

THEODOR FONTANE (1819–1898)

writer, journalist

Theodor Fontane was born in Neuruppin, Germany. He first made contact with literary circles when he worked in Berlin as a chemist. Later he became a newspaper reporter and was a war correspondent during the Prussian wars. He wrote this letter to his six-year-old son during his time as foreign correspondent in London, 1855–1859.

London
25 January 1857

My dear George,

Your pencil drawing reached me yesterday and pleased me very much. The people are of a singular portrait-likeness of themselves and encourage the greatest hopes. If you are to be to painters what your father is to poets you will earn a good living as a nightwatchman. I should certainly have recognised the preacher you drew as such, if only he did not look so much like a babe wrapped in swaddling clothes. This is perhaps very perceptive of you, and a little mischievous; you look upon clergymen as God's babes-in-arms whilst the rest of us grow up a little less well tended and are allowed to run wild – As for the coming into leaf of your trees you have found a happy solution, you draw them before it happens and present us instead with a single bud that, judging by its thickness, contains the whole splendour of spring. Who is there to say that the leaves it contains do not beat everything produced in landscape painting to date? – you pay special attention to the 'hotel', of this I approve. Smoke rises from two chimneys suggesting good food, bottle and glass are placed in the street and seem to indicate the proprietor as being a splendid man, who does not worry when a diner breaks a plate. I am not quite clear about the two trees of which one grows on the second floor, the other one right on the roof; but does everything have to be clear? What nonsense! All greatness is shrouded in darkness and all darkness (only it must be VERY dark) may boast of the greatness it contains; we shall exchange our thoughts about this topic verbally.

Remember me to your Mama and Grandmama as well as young Theodor and stand by your art. As always,

Your Father

Theodor Fontane

HARRIET BEECHER STOWE (1811–1896)
author

Harriet Beecher Stowe was born into a prominent family of American preachers and herself married an ordained theological professor. She sprang to fame with her anti-slavery novel, *Uncle Tom's Cabin*. When she met Abraham Lincoln during the Civil War he remarked, 'So this is the little woman who brought on this big war.' She wrote the following letter to her daughter Georgiana, then sixteen, soon after the death of her eldest son, Henry.

February 12, 1859

My dear Georgie, – Why haven't I written? Because, dear Georgie, I am like the dry, dead, leafless tree, and have only cold, dead, slumbering buds of hope on the end of stiff, hard frozen twigs of thought, but no leaves, no blossoms; nothing to send a little girl who doesn't know what to do with herself any more than a kitten. I am cold, weary, dead; everything is a burden to me.

I let my plants die by inches before my eyes, and do not water them, and dread everything I do, and wish it was not to be done, and so when I get a letter from my little girl I smile and say, 'Dear little puss, I will answer it'; and I sit hour after hour with folded hands, looking at the inkstand and dreading to begin. The fact is, pussy, mamma is tired. Life to you is gay and joyous, but to mamma it has been a battle in which the spirit is willing but the flesh weak, and she would be glad, like the woman in the St. Bernard, to lie down with her arms around the wayside cross, and sleep away into a brighter scene. Henry's fair, sweet face looks down upon me now and then from out a cloud, and I feel again all the bitterness of the eternal 'No' which says I must never, never, in this life, see that face, lean on that arm, hear that voice.

Not that my faith in God in the least fails, and that I do not believe that all this is for good. I do, and though not happy, I am blessed. Weak, weary as I am, I rest on Jesus in the innermost depth of my soul, and am quite sure that there is coming an inconceivable hour of beauty and glory when I shall regain Jesus, and he will give me back my beloved one, whom he is educating in a far higher sphere than I proposed. So do not mistake me, – only know that mamma is sitting weary by the wayside, feeling weak and worn, but in no sense discouraged.

Your affectionate mother,

H.B.S.

LOUISA MAY ALCOTT (1832–1888)

writer

L. M. Alcott was born in Pennsylvania, the daughter of devoutly Christian, unworldly parents. She helped support the family from an early age by writing blood-and-thunder magazine stories. In her mid-thirties, drawing on childhood memories, she wrote the enormously successful *Little Women*, a year in the life of Meg (sixteen), Jo (fifteen, the budding author), Beth (thirteen), and Amy (twelve), and the rich, delightful boy-over-the-way, Laurie (fifteen). She is writing to nephews, aged twelve and ten, the sons of her eldest sister Ann (Meg in the book). By the time this letter was written, both *Little Women* and *Little Men* had been published.

New York Dec. 4, 1875

Dear Fred and Donny, – We went to see the newsboys, and I wish you'd been with us, it was so interesting. A nice big house has been built for them, with dining-room and kitchen on the first floor, bath-rooms and school-room next, two big sleeping-places, – third and fourth stories, – and at the top a laundry and gymnasium. We saw all the tables set for breakfast, – a plate and bowl for each, – and in the kitchen great kettles, four times as big as our copper boiler, for tea and coffee, soup, and meat. They have bread and meat and coffee for breakfast, and bread and cheese and tea for supper, and get their own dinners out. School was just over when we got there, and one hundred and eighty boys were in the immense room with desks down the middle, and all around the walls were little cupboards numbered. Each boy on coming in gives his name, pays six cents, gets a key, and puts away his hat, books, and jacket (if he has 'em) in his own cubby for the night. They pay five cents for supper, and schooling, baths, etc., are free. They were a smart-looking set, larking around in shirts and trousers, barefooted, but the faces were clean, and heads smooth, and clothes pretty decent; yet they support themselves, for not one of them has any parents or home but this. One little chap, only 6, was trotting round as busy as a bee, locking up his small shoes and ragged jacket as if they were great treasures. I asked about little Pete, and the man told us his brother, only nine, supported him and took care of him entirely; and wouldn't let Pete be sent away to any home, because he wished to have 'his family' with him.

Think of that Fred! How would it seem to be all alone in a big city, with no mamma to cuddle you; no two grandpa's houses to take you in; not a penny but what you earned, and Donny to take care of? Could you do it? Nine-year-old Patsey does it capitally; buys Pete's clothes, pays for his bed and supper, and puts pennies in the savings-bank. There's a brave little man for you! I wanted to see him; but he is a newsboy, and sells late papers, because, though harder work, it pays better, and the coast is clear for those who do it.

The savings-bank was a great table full of slits, each one leading to a little place below and numbered outside, so each boy knew his own. Once a month the bank is opened, and the lads take out what they like, or have it invested in a big bank for them to have when they find homes out West, as many do, and make good farmers. One boy was putting in some pennies as we looked, and I asked how much he had saved this month. 'Fourteen dollars, ma'am,' says the 13-year-older, proudly slipping in the last cent. A prize of $3 is offered to the lad who saves the most in a month.

The beds upstairs were in two immense rooms, ever so much larger than our town hall, – one hundred in one, and one hundred and eighty in another, – all narrow beds with a blue quilt, neat pillow, and clean sheet. They are built in long rows, one over another, and the upper boy has to climb up as on board ship. I'd have liked to see one hundred and eighty all in their 'by-lows' at once, and I asked the man if they didn't train when all were in. 'Lord, ma'am, they're up at five, poor little chaps, and are so tired at night that they drop off right away. Now and then some boy kicks up a little row, but we have a watchman, and he soon settles 'em.'

He also told me how that very day a neat, smart young man came in, and said he was one of their boys who went West with a farmer only a little while ago; and now he owned eighty acres of land, had a good house, and was doing well, and had come to New York to find his sister, and to take her away to live with him. Wasn't that nice? Lots of boys do as well. Instead of loafing round the streets and getting into mischief, they are taught to be tidy, industrious, and honest, and then sent away into the wholesome country to support themselves.

It was funny to see 'em scrub in the bath-room, – feet and faces, – comb their hair, fold up their clothes in the dear cubbies, which make them so happy because they feel that they *own* something.

The man said every boy wanted one, even though he had neither shoes nor jacket to put in it; but would lay away an old rag of a cap or a dirty tippet with an air of satisfaction fine to see. Some lads sat reading, and the man said they loved it so they'd read all night, if allowed. At nine he gave the word 'Bed!' and away went the lads, trooping up to sleep in shirts and trousers, as nightgowns are not provided. How would a boy I know like that, – a boy who likes to have 'trommin' on his nighties? Of course, I don't mean dandy Don! Oh, dear no!

After nine (if late in coming in) they are fined five cents; after ten, ten cents, and after eleven they can't come in at all. This makes them steady, keeps them out of harm, and gives them time for study. Some go to the theatre, and sleep anywhere; some sleep at the Home, but go out for a better breakfast than they get there, as the swell ones are fond of goodies, and live well in their funny way. Coffee and cakes at Fulton Market is 'the tip-top grub,' and they often spend all their day's earnings in a play and a supper, and sleep in boxes or cellars after it.

Lots of pussies were round the kitchen; and one black one I called a bootblack, and a gray kit that yowled loud was a newsboy. That made some chaps laugh, and they nodded at me as I went out. Nice boys! but I know some nicer ones. Write and tell me something about my poor Squabby.

By-by, your
WEEDY

ANTON PAVLOVICH CHEKHOV (1860–1904)

author and dramatist

Chekhov's father, Pavel, was the son of a liberated serf who owned a grocery store in the run-down port of Taganrog on the Sea of Azov. Pavel, a strange, tyrannical man, frequently beat his six children, sincerely thinking to do them good. He was obsessed by the rituals of the Russian Orthodox Church and spent hours rehearsing these ceremonies while his children were obliged to man the cold, dark grocer's shop. The eldest two fled to Moscow, followed by Pavel, when business was bankrupted, and the rest of the children except Anton, who was given a corner of his old home as a refuge in return for services to the new owner. He remained there until he was nineteen.

He writes to his youngest brother, Mikhail, who was to be a writer, publisher, translator and Anton's biographer.

Taganrog
between April 6 and 8, 1879

Dear Brother Misha,

I got your letter while sitting around yawning by the gate at the height of a horrible fit of boredom, so you can imagine how perfectly timed it seemed – and so enormous too. You have a good handwriting, and I didn't find a single grammatical error anywhere in the letter. There is one thing I don't like, though. Why do you refer to yourself as my 'worthless, insignificant little brother'? So you are aware of your worthlessness, are you? Not all Mishas have to be identical, you know. Do you know where you should be aware of your worthlessness? Before God, perhaps, or before human intelligence, before beauty or nature. But not before people. Among people you should be aware of your worth. You're no cheat, you're an honest man, aren't you? Well then, respect yourself for being a good honest fellow. Don't confuse 'humility' with 'an awareness of your own worthlessness.' Gregory [a cousin] has grown. He's a nice boy. I often play knucklebones with him. He's received your packages. You do well to read books. Get into the habit of reading. You'll come to appreciate it in time. So Madame Beecher Stowe brought tears to your eyes? I thumbed through her once and read her straight through for scholarly purposes six months ago, and when I was done I experienced that unpleasant sensation that mortals are wont to feel when they've eaten too many raisins or dried currants. The hawfinch I promised you has escaped, and little is known of his present place of residence. I'll figure out something else to bring you. Take a look at the following books: <u>Don Quixote</u> (complete, in all seven or eight parts). It's a fine work written by Cervantes, who is placed on just about the level of Shakespeare. I recommend Turgenev's <u>Hamlet and Don Quixote</u> to our brothers if they haven't read it already. As for you, you wouldn't understand it. If you feel like reading an entertaining travelogue, try Goncharov's <u>Frigate Pallada</u>, etc. I send Masha special regards. Don't all of you feel bad that I'm coming late. Time flies no matter how bored you brag you are. I'm bringing a lodger along who will pay twenty rubles a month and be under our personal supervision. I'll soon be off for a bargaining session with his mother. Pray for my success! However, even twenty rubles is not much, considering Moscow prices and Mother's character – she'll give him good honest food. Our teachers get three hundred & fifty rubles a head, and they feed the poor boys on the blood dripping from their roasts, like dogs.

A. Chekhov

MARIANNE THORNTON (1797–1887)

Marianne Thornton was E.M. Forster's great-aunt, and although he was only seven when she died, he was to say, 'She and no one else made my career as a writer possible, and her love, in a most tangible sense, followed me beyond the grave.'

Miss Thornton was a rich Anglican who was against slavery and campaigned in favour of public education. When Forster's father died, the child was one year old. Edward Morgan replaced him as Aunt Monie's favourite nephew. In her will she left him £8,000, the interest on which was to educate him. He became one of the most distinguished but least prolific of twentieth-century novelists. Long after he had given up fiction he wrote a biography of his great-aunt which concluded with a series of nine letters from her to him.

May 6th 1880

My dear Morgan I send you a gardener's apron for working in the garden, nothing will improve your appetite like being a Gardener, so intelligent as you are you will soon be Aunt Laura's head man. Tell her I went to my garden, that is my school, and staid two hours there. I had my wheeled chair taken there and was rolled about and the children laughed and I don't wonder. –

Ever your affectionate MONIE.

The third in the series describes 'a scene which occurred at the opening of Parliament in the year 1804'. Forster was given to understand that this was an accurate description.

Dear Mr Morgan

I hope you will do me the favour of accepting a dozen of hyacinths that will all blow and grow in glasses in water – Lloyd of course is full of glasses, price half-nothing, but you could if you liked put them in earth in pots. What stupid names they give the poor things. I wish I could think of some better ones. I have just stuck the names on my glasses but I am sure you would find better.

I think its time now for you to write me another letter. Do you write every day. I can show you a big thick copy book that when I was just your age I wrote for my father. He had not very good eyes and could not write much himself, and I was so proud of being able to help him. And what do you think he did to reward me. Why, poor old George the Third was coming to summon parliament. That means he ordered that all the members of parliament were to come to hear what he had got to say to them about making new laws and altering the old. He was a good man and wanted to do right, but he was very obstinate and used to get very angry and at last very ill, and he quite lost his senses and kept calling the people about him peacocks. When the day came for him to meet his faithful commons though very ill he insisted on having his own way so they gave it him, and he went, and I could see his carriage – all gold and glass, and I did so beg of my papa to let me go across Palace Yard and he carried me across and took me into the House of Commons, and they were ordered by the Lords to meet the King and hear what he had to say to us. And there he was sitting on his Throne with his King's Crown on, his robes scarlet velvet and ermine, held up his speech written out for just what he had to say. But Oh dear he stood up and made a bow and began 'My Lords and Peacocks'. The people who were not fond of him laughed, the people who did love him cried, and he went back to be no longer a King, and his eldest son reigned in his stead and Regent Street was named after him.

This is a very dull letter so I will finish.

Your affectionate old

AUNT MONIE

'Dull letter?' writes Forster. 'I wish I could get many like it or write any like it! What a sequence – hyacinth bulbs, copybook, mad King! How much has died with her which, properly evoked, might have lived!'

He introduces the letter given next as 'a comedy'.

My dear Morgan

Two such nasty men came here last night and peeped in at the kitchen window and saw all the maids eating their suppers. Did you ever look at what is called a safe in which Sarah Cook keeps her meat? It is something like a very very big birdcage only the sides are canvas, and it hangs in the passage that leads from the Common on to the garden. Mrs Reed my night nurse always comes to supper, but as she got to the door of the dark passage, she met two men coming out, but it was so dark she could not see them but one was bigger than the other.

This morning I was half asleep but was soon quite awake, Sarah Cook crying with all her heart and saying, 'Oh mam I have something so dreadful to tell you' – 'Oh do make haste,' says I, for I began to be afraid that the maids had all gone and drowned themselves in the Long Pond. – Oh no says she, but it *is* dreadful – 2 thieves have broken open the safe and taken off three chickens and a leg of mutton, and then she sobbed and cried as if she would never get over it. So I scolded her and said it wasn't dreadful, and then Aunt Emmy said she would send to Weymouth to get us some more mutton and some more chickens, and so we should not be the worse off. I don't think anyone has such an aunt Emmy as you and I have.

We had a man called a detective to help us to find out the thieves but he fears we cant though he thinks he knows who they are. When he came into the room he said, 'Good day ladies I hear you had some unpleasant visitors last night – but tell your maids always to shut the shutters and not let the world see what they are about.' This is good advice I have no doubt. He went away saying 'You shall have my best attention ladies in any further alarm.'

From your AUNT MONIE

Her last letter to him was one of mild astonishment. It was the summer of 1887 and the occasion of Queen Victoria's Jubilee. Forster explains: 'Following the lead of my mother and other respectable citizens I was violently anti-Jubilee . . . my grandmother and I planned to spend the day together in strict seclusion . . . Aunt Monie . . . rebuked my attitude and recommended deference, though I do not feel her arguments for monarchy very sound.'

My dear Morgan – I thought you would like this little geography book by which it seems you can always find your way about. The sun they say always is shining on some bit of the globe that belongs to *us* meaning by us all English people – and that reminds me that I heard you did not like the Queen – but I think that must be because you do not know her, neither do I as an acquaintance, but I do know she is the best Queen or King we have ever had. She has kept her crown on her head while everyone in Europe has had theirs shaken. Then she is the only King or Queen who has been saving – always paying everybody all she owes them – and she is so kind and full of pity for those who are ill and in trouble. – Absolute governors who do not care for the law, but help themselves to their neighbours goods – if she took to those sort of ways – why we should soon learn to be thankful for her, but I must end now for Dr Spitta has made me buy some little pots of tallow to be lighted up tomorrow – from
Your dear old AUNT MONIE

In the event Forster's republicanism feebly gave way. He sat on a wall with other children to watch the procession. At the critical moment, feeling a policeman's eye on him, he took off his hat and waved it along with the rest.

MARK TWAIN (1835–1910)

novelist and humorist

Mark Twain's real name was Samuel Langhorne Clemens; Mark Twain, in river language, means 'two fathoms deep' and derives from the time the writer worked as a pilot on the Mississippi. He is chiefly remembered for two semi-autobiographical works, *The Adventures of Huckleberry Finn* and *The Adventures of Tom Sawyer*. Two of his daughters and his wife predeceased him. When they were a family they loved to have a 'family Christmas'. In his role of Father Christmas he addresses a long and important letter to his eldest daughter Susie.

Palace of St. Nicholas
In the Moon
Christmas Morning

My dear Susie Clemens,

I have received and read all the letters which you and your little sister have written by the hand of your mother and your nurses; I have also read those which you little people have written me with your own hands – for although you did not use any characters that are in grown peoples' alphabet, you used the characters that all children in all lands on earth and in the twinkling stars use; and as all my subjects in the moon are children and use no characters but that, you will easily understand that I can read your and your baby sister's jagged and fantastic marks without any trouble at all. But I had trouble with those letters which you dictated through your mother and the nurses, for I am a foreigner and cannot read English writing well. You will find that I made no mistakes about the things which you and the baby ordered in your *own* letters – I went down your chimney at midnight when you were asleep and delivered them all myself – and kissed both of you, too, because you are good children, well-trained, nice-mannered, and about the most obedient little people I ever saw. But in the letters which you dictated there were some words which I could not make out for certain, and one or two small orders which I could not fill because we ran out of stock. Our last lot of kitchen-furniture for dolls has just gone to a very poor little child in the North Star away up in the cold country above the Big Dipper. Your mama can show you that star and you will say, 'Little Snow Flake' (for that is the child's name) 'I'm glad you got that furniture, for you need it more than I.' That is, you must *write* that with your own hand, and Snow Flake will write you an answer. If you only spoke it she wouldn't hear you. Make your letter light and thin, for the distance is great and the postage very heavy.

There was a word or two in your mama's letter which I couldn't be certain of. I took it to be 'trunk full of doll's clothes.' Is that it? I will call at your kitchen door about nine o'clock this morning to inquire. But I must not see anybody and I must not speak to anybody but you. When the kitchen doorbell rings George must be blindfolded and sent to open the door. Then he must go back to the dining-room or the china closet and take the cook with him. You must tell George he must walk on tiptoe and not speak – otherwise he will die some day. Then you must go up to the nursery and stand on a chair or the nurse's bed and put your ear to the speaking tube that leads down to the kitchen and when I whistle through it you must speak in the tube and say, 'Welcome, Santa Claus!' Then I will ask whether it was a trunk you ordered or not. If you say it was, I shall ask you what *color* you want the trunk to be. Your mama will help you to name a nice color and then you must tell me every single thing in detail which you want the trunk to contain. Then when I say 'Good bye and a Merry Christmas to my little Susie Clemens,' you must say, 'Good bye, good old Santa Claus, I thank you very much and please tell that little Snow Flake I will look at her star tonight and she must look down here' – I will be right in the West bay-window; and every fine night I will look at her star and say, 'I know somebody up there and *like* her, too.' Then you must go down into the library and make George close all the doors that open into the main hall, and everybody must keep still for a little while. I will go to the moon and get those things and in a few minutes I will come down the chimney that belongs to the fireplace that is in the hall – if it is a trunk you want – because I couldn't get such a thing as a trunk down the nursery chimney, you know.

People may talk if they want, until they hear my footsteps in the hall.

Then you tell them to keep quiet a little while till I go back up the chimney. Maybe you will not hear my footsteps at all – so you may go now and then and peep through the dining-room doors, and by and by you will see that thing which you want, right under the piano in the drawing-room – for I shall put it there. If I should leave any snow in the hall, you must tell George to sweep it into the fireplace, for I haven't time to do such things. George must not use a broom but a rag – else he will die some day. You must watch George and not let him run into danger. If my boot should leave a stain on the marble, George must not holy-stone it away. Leave it there always in memory of my visit; and whenever you look at it or show it to anybody you must let it remind you to be a good little girl. Whenever you are naughty and somebody points to that mark which your good old Santa Claus's boot made on the marble, what will you say, little Sweetheart?

Good bye for a few minutes, till I come down to the world and ring the kitchen door-bell.

Your loving
Santa Claus

Whom people sometimes call 'The Man in the Moon.'

COLONEL GEORGE WHITE (1835–1912)
later Field-Marshal

In the nineteenth century the British Army had its garrisons through-out the world, and not only in imperial territory. Colonel George White had won his VC when he took the pass above Kabul in Afghanistan by ignoring superior orders. (He wrote to his wife: 'I thought these orders rot, and put them in my pocket.') Later we find him garrisoned in Egypt, just after the death of General Gordon and the capture of Khartoum by the Sudanese army of the Mahdi. These events induced in many British people an intense jingoism. The colonel reckoned that he was only a very moderate jingo. Here is a letter to his daughter, aged four.

In the land of Egypt
24th April 1885

My dear Rosie,

I know a little lady far away to whom a letter is owed since I had to dwell among the wicked Egyptians, I am sitting down on oh! such a small stool, on oh! such a hot day, to write her a letter. I am building a home on the banks of the Nile, and the black men who ought to be working very hard are sitting down under a tree doing nothing. If I go out and scold them, they don't understand me, and it makes me very hot, so I have to look on at the lazy fellows, and hope they will do a little work when the sun is not quite so hot.

We had a black gentleman to dine with us. His name is Kasm-el-Mons, and he was a great friend of Gen. Gordon's and fought for him as long as he could. He rode into our Camp with a great many followers beating drums. Some of the men were riding on donkeys, and some rode on camels, & some on horses. The men on horses rode as fast as they can, flourishing their spears as if they were fighting their enemies, and they all made such a grand show that the English soldiers thought it was the Mahdi come to make peace . . . I cannot send you any more photographs as there is not a shop within 120 miles of where I am . . .

Your loving Father

WILLIAM JAMES (1842–1910)

philosopher

William James's great-grandfather, grandfather and uncle were also called William James; so was his second son. His father, his brother (the renowned novelist) and his first-born were all called Henry. From his father, a Swedenborgian who wrote on theology, came his interest in belief. He became a professor of philosophy, and later psychology, at Harvard. He was essentially a pragmatist and wrote a book on the subject in 1907; another major work was *Varieties of Religious Experience* (1902).

To his son Henry, aged eight, sent with brother William, sister Margaret Mary and their German governess to the more benign climate of South Carolina, he writes:

Cambridge
Mar. 27 [1888]

Beloved Heinrich, – Your long letter came yesterday *p.m.* Much the best you ever writ, and the address on the envelope so well written that I wondered whose hand it was, and never thought it might be yours. Your tooth also was a precious memorial – I hope you'll get a better one in its place. Send me the other as soon as it is tookin out. They ought to go into the Peabody Museum. If any of George Washington's baby-teeth had been kept till now, they would be put somewhere in a public museum for the world to wonder at. I will keep this tooth, so that, if you grow up to be a second Geo. Washington, I may sell it to a Museum. When Washington was only eight years old his mother did n't know he was going to be Washington. But he did be it, when the time came . . .

Now pray, old Harry, stick to your books and let me see you do sums and read *fast* when you get back.

The best of all of us is your mother, though.

Goodbye!

Your loving Dad.

W.J.

To his son, Alexander.

Berkeley, Cal., Aug. 28, 1898

Darling OLD Cherubini, – See how brave this girl and boy are in the Yosemite Valley! [*Photograph of a boy and girl standing on a rock which hangs dizzily over a great precipice above the Yosemite Valley.*] I saw a moving sight the other morning before breakfast in a little hotel where I slept in the dusty fields. The young man of the house had shot a little wolf called a coyote in the early morning. The heroic little animal lay on the ground, with his big furry ears, and his clean white teeth, and his jolly cheerful little body, but his brave little life was gone. It made me think how brave all these living things are. Here little coyote was, without any clothes or house or books or anything, with nothing but his own naked self to pay his way with, and risking his life so cheerfully – and losing it – just to see if he could pick up a meal near the hotel. He was doing his coyote-business like a hero, and you must do your boy-business, and I my man-business bravely too, or else we won't be worth as much as that little coyote. Your mother can find a picture of him in those green books of animals, and I want you to copy it. Your loving

Dad

To his daughter, aged thirteen, living with English friends at Harrow, and suffering homesickness.

Villa Luise,
Bad-Naueim May 26, 1900

Darling Peg, – Your letter came last night and explained sufficiently the cause
of your long silence. You have evidently been in a bad state of spirits again,
and dissatisfied with your environment; and I judge that you have been still
more dissatisfied with the inner state of trying to consume your own smoke,
and grin and bear it, so as to carry out your mother's behests made after the
time when you scared us so by your inexplicable tragic outcries in those
earlier letters. Well! I believe you have been trying to do the manly thing
under difficult circumstances, but one learns only gradually to do the *best*
thing; and the best thing for you would be to write at least weekly, if only a
post-card, and say just how things are going. If you are in bad spirits, there
is no harm whatever in communicating that fact, and defining the character
of it, or describing it as exactly as you like. The bad thing is to pour out the
contents of one's bad spirits on others and leave them with it, as it were, on
their hands, as if it was for them to do something about it. That was what
you did in your other letter which alarmed us so, for your shrieks of anguish
were so excessive, and so unexplained by anything you told us in the way of
facts, that we did n't know but what you had suddenly gone crazy. That is
the *worst* sort of thing you can do. The middle sort of thing is what you do
this time – namely, keep silent for more than a fortnight, and when you do
write, still write rather mysteriously about your sorrows, not being quite
open enough.

Now, my dear little girl, you have come to an age when the inward life
develops and when some people (and on the whole those who have most of
a destiny) find that all is not a bed of roses. Among other things there will
be waves of terrible sadness, which last sometimes for days; and
dissatisfaction with one's self, and irritation at others, and anger at
circumstances and stony insensibility, etc., etc., which taken together form a
melancholy. Now, painful as it is, this is sent to us for an enlightenment. It
always passes off, and we learn about life from it, and we ought to learn a
great many good things if we react on it rightly. (For instance, you learn how
good a thing your home is, and your country, and your brothers, and you
may learn to be more considerate of other people, who, you now learn, may
have their inner weaknesses and sufferings, too.) Many persons take a kind
of sickly delight in hugging it; and some sentimental ones may even be
proud of it, as showing a fine sorrowful kind of sensibility. Such persons

make a regular habit of the luxury of woe. That is the worst possible reaction on it. It is usually a sort of disease, when we get it strong, arising from the organism having generated some poison in the blood; and we must n't submit to it an hour longer than we can help, but jump at every chance to attend to anything cheerful or comic or take part in anything active that will divert us from our mean, pining inward state of feeling. When it passes off, as I said, we know more than we did before. And we must try to make it last as short a time as possible. The worst of it often is that, while we are in it, we don't *want* to get out of it. We hate it, and yet we prefer staying in it – that is a part of the disease. If we find ourselves like that, we must make ourselves do something different, go with people, speak cheerfully, set ourselves to some hard work, make ourselves sweat, etc.; and that is the good way of reacting that makes of us a valuable character. The disease makes you think of *yourself* all the time; and the way out of it is to keep as busy as we can thinking of *things* and *other people* – no matter what's the matter with our self.

I have no doubt that you are doing as well as you know how, darling little Peg; but we have to learn everything, and I also have no doubt that you'll manage it better and better if you ever have any more of it, and soon it will fade away, simply leaving you with more experience. The great thing for you *now*, I should suppose, would be to enter as friendlily as possible into the interest of the Clarke children. If you like them, or acted as if you liked them, you need n't trouble about the question of whether they like you or not. They probably will, fast enough; and if they don't, it will be their funeral, not yours. But this is a great lecture, so I will stop. The great thing about it is that it is all true.

The baths are threatening to disagree with me again, so I may stop them soon. Will let you know as quick as anything is decided. Good news from home: the Merrimans have taken the Irving Street house for another year, and the Wambaughs (of the Law School) have taken Chocurua, though at a reduced rent. The weather here is almost continuously cold and sunless. Your mother is sleeping, and will doubtless add a word to this when she wakes. Keep a merry heart – 'time and the hour run through the roughest day' – and believe me ever your most loving

W.J.

LORD AND LADY RANDOLPH CHURCHILL

LADY RANDOLPH CHURCHILL (1854–1921)
Mother of Winston Spencer Churchill

At one time dubbed 'the greatest living Englishman', Sir Winston Churchill was, in fact, on his mother's side, half American. Jennie Jerome was the beautiful, headstrong daughter of an American financier who, in 1874, married Lord Randolph Churchill. Their home was Blenheim Palace. There Winston was born, six weeks prematurely, after a December ball at which his mother (still, after all, only twenty) had been energetically dancing.

Here Lady Randolph writes to Winston when he was at Harrow where he could not, or would not, apply himself to any subject in which he was not interested. (Jack is his younger brother, Everest his much-loved nurse.)

2 Connaught Place
Thursday 12 June 1890

Dearest Winston,

I am sending this by Everest, who is going to see how you are getting on. I would go down to you – but I have so many things to arrange about the Ascot party next week that I can't manage it. I have much to say to you, I'm afraid not of a pleasant nature. You know darling, how I hate to find fault with you, but I can't help myself this time . . . In the first place your Father is very angry with you for not acknowledging the gift of 5£ for a whole week, and then writing an offhand careless letter.

Your report which I enclose is as you will see a *very* bad one. You work in such a fitful inharmonious way, that you are bound to come out last – look at your place in the form! Yr Father & I are both more disappointed than we can say, that you are not able to go up for yr preliminary Exam: I daresay you have 1000 excuses for not doing so – but there the fact remains! If only you had a better place in your form, & were a little more methodical I would *try* & find an excuse for you. Dearest Winston, you make me very unhappy – I had built up such hopes about you & felt so proud of you – & now all is gone. My only consolation is that your conduct is good, & that you are an affectionate son – but your work is an insult to your intelligence. If you would only trace out a plan of action for yourself & Carry it out & be *determined* to do so – I am sure you could accomplish anything you wished. It is that thoughtlessness of yours which is your greatest enemy. Your Father threatens to send you with a tutor off somewhere for the holidays – I can assure you it will take a great deal to pacify him, & I do not know how it is to be done. I must say I think you repay his kindness to you very badly. There is Jack on the other hand – who comes out at the head of his class every week – not withstanding his bad eye.

I will say no more now – but Winston you are old enough to see how serious this is to you – & how the next year or two & the use you make of them, will affect your whole life – stop and think it out for yourself & take a good pull before it is too late. You know dearest boy that I will always help you all I can.

Your loving but distressed
Mother

LORD RANDOLPH CHURCHILL (1849–1895), Aristocrat, politician

Winston Churchill's father was the third son of the 7th duke of Marlborough. He had a brief parliamentary career in which he rose to become Chancellor of the Exchequer. At thirty-seven, people saw in him a future prime minister. Suddenly everything crumpled. He quarrelled with his colleagues, his political judgement faltered, a mental malady brought about his death in 1895. Between resigning from the House of Commons and his death he travelled abroad in search of renewed health.

Johannesburg
27 June 1891

Dearest Winston,

You cannot think how pleased I was to get your interesting & well written letter & to learn that you were getting on well. I understand that Mr. Welldon thinks you will be able to pass your examination into the army when the time comes. I hope it may be so, as it will be a tremendous pull for you ultimately. I have been having a most agreeable travel in this very remarkable country. I expect that when you are my age you will see S Africa to be the most populous & wealthy of all our colonies. I suppose Mama has read you my letters & that you have seen my letters in the *Daily Graphic*, for I cannot tell you more than I have already written. You would have enjoyed an expedition I made last week for shooting purposes. A regular gipsy life, sleeping on a mattress in a bell tent, dressing and washing in the open air & eating round a camp fire. The sport was vy fair & wild & there was much variety of game to shoot. Here I have been examining gold mines & investing money in what I hope will be fortunate undertakings for I expect you & Jack will be a couple of expensive articles to keep as you grow older.

Tomorrow we start for our journey up country staying a few days at Pretoria on the way. My waggons have been slowly treking up through Bechuanaland with Captain Giles, Rayner & the others since the middle of May & ought to be now at Fort Juli in Matabele Land where I hope to join them in about 10 or 12 days. I expect that we shall be vy comfortable & jolly when we get to the waggons. I have not had any roughing it or discomfort yet, as we have always been put up by friends and have avoided the Hotels which are most dirty & uncomfortable. We have a six or seven days journey before us from Pretoria to Juli. We travel in a 'spider' a sort of light framed waggonette with eight mules, and go about 50 miles in the day.

The accommodation on the road for the night is said to be vy indifferent. I suppose this will just reach you as you are going home for the holidays. I hope you will have a good time at Banstead & that you and Jack will amuse yourself well. Give him my vy best love & tell him how glad I am to hear of his good place in the school. Perhaps he will write to me before long. Goodbye take care of yourself, don't give Mama any trouble.

Ever yr most affte father
RANDOLPH S. CHURCHILL

I am doubtful about being able to bring home a tame antelope. The Bechuanaland stamps I think I can obtain: I have a pointer called Charlie & a shooting pony called Charlie both excellent animals. When we travel we always have our guns ready to secure any game which may show itself.

ROBERT LOUIS STEVENSON (1850–1894)

novelist and poet

Robert Louis Stevenson wrote and published prolifically and success-fully for all ages in the course of his short, often invalid life. In his last years he sailed to the South Seas where, all too briefly, he recovered his health before dying of a haemorrhage. In addition to those lasting works such as *Treasure Island, Kidnapped* and *A Child's Garden of Verses*, he wrote a spirited account of the life of Father Damien, the Belgian priest who cared so much for lepers that he succumbed to their disease.

Here are two letters to young correspondents.

Annie Ide, daughter of a friend, H.C. Ide, felt deprived of a birthday in her own right, having been born on Christmas Day. Stevenson sent a formal document to her father, giving the child his own birthday and, in effect, adopting her. She is also to add the name Louisa to Annie H. Subsequently he writes to her . . .

Vailima Samoa [November 1891]

MY DEAR LOUISA, – Your picture of the church, the photograph of yourself and your sister, and your very witty and pleasing letter, came all in a bundle, and made me feel I had my money's worth for that birthday. I am now, I must be, one of your nearest relatives; exactly what we are to each other, I do not know, I doubt if the case has ever happened before – your papa ought to know, and I don't believe he does; but I think I ought to call you in the meanwhile, and until we get the advice of counsel learned in the law, my name-daughter. Well, I was extremely pleased to see by the church that my name-daughter could draw; by the letter, that she was no fool; and by the photograph, that she was a pretty girl, which hurts nothing. See how virtues are rewarded! My first idea of adopting you was entirely charitable; and here I find that I am quite proud of it, and of you, and that I chose just the kind of name-daughter I wanted. For I can draw too, or rather I mean to say I could before I forgot how; and I am very far from being a fool myself, however much I may look it; and I am as beautiful as the day, or at least I once hoped that perhaps I might be going to be. And so I might. So that you see we are well met, and peers on these important points. I am very glad also that you are older than your sister. So should I have been, if I had had one. So that the number of points and virtues which you have inherited from your name-father is already quite surprising.

I wish you would tell your father – not that I like to encourage my rival – that we have had a wonderful time here of late, and that they are having a cold day on Mulinuu, and the consuls are writing reports, and I am writing to the *Times*, and if we don't get rid of our friends this time I shall begin to despair of everything but my name-daughter.

You are quite wrong as to the effect of the birthday on your age. From the moment the deed was registered (as it was in the public press with every solemnity), the 13th of November became your own *and only* birthday, and you ceased to have been born on Christmas Day. Ask your father: I am sure he will tell you this is sound law. You are thus become a month and twelve days younger than you were, but will go on growing older for the future in the regular and human manner from one 13th November to the next. The effect on me is more doubtful; I may, as you suggest, live for ever; I might, on the other hand, come to pieces like the one-horse shay at a moment's notice; doubtless the step was risky, but I do not the least regret that which enables me to sign myself your revered and delighted name-father,

ROBERT LOUIS STEVENSON

To Ned Orr, an American boy who had written for an autograph.

> Vailima Upolu Samoa 28th
> November 1891

DEAR SIR, – Your obliging communication is to hand. I am glad to find
that you have read some of my books, and to see that you spell my name
right. This is a point (for some reason) of great difficulty; and I believe that
a gentleman who can spell Stevenson with a v at sixteen, should have a show
for the Presidency before fifty. By that time
                         I, nearer to the wayside inn
predict that you will have outgrown your taste for autographs, but perhaps
your son may have inherited the collection, and on the morning of the great
day will recall my prophecy to your mind. And in the papers of 1921 (say)
this letter may arouse a smile.

   Whatever you do, read something else besides novels and newspapers; the
first are good enough when they are good; the second, at their best, are
worth nothing. Read great books of literature and history; try to understand
the Roman Empire and the Middle Ages; be sure you do not understand
when you dislike them; condemnation is non-comprehension. And if you
know something of these two periods, you will know a little more about
today, and may be a good President.

   I send you my best wishes, and am yours,

                         ROBERT LOUIS STEVENSON
                         Author of a vast quantity of little books.

THE REVEREND EDWARD LAMBURN (d. 1915)

curate and schoolmaster

Edward Lamburn and his wife Clara Crompton had three children, Mary Gwendolen (Gwen), Richmal and John Battersby Crompton (Jack). He trained as a curate but settled as a schoolmaster in Lancashire. His enthusiasm for learning was passed to Gwen and Richmal, who were intelligent, studious, and law-abiding. Jack was tutored at home by his father, and his enthusiasm for all the dubious exploits a boy could get embroiled in were to inspire Richmal to write the William Brown stories whose popularity still endures. In this letter to Gwen, her father reproves his elder daughter – with extreme tenderness – for a moral peccadillo (as he sees it). If William was based on Jack, Mr Lamburn was certainly not the model for Mr Brown.

My darling little Gwen,

Thank you very much for the kind birthday wishes that I received yesterday . . .

It would be much nicer if you did not pass such severe strictures upon others especially those who are older than yourself. She may be stuck up; or it may be that you do not understand her. But Our Lord's command Matth. VII 1 is 'Judge not, that ye be not judged.' . . . The habit of evil-speaking grows on one unless it be effectually checked to much misery & unhappiness in the world . . . If we all knew how much our words affected others, I think we should become changed beings . . .

I am afraid you will think I have been scolding you, my darling; but I have really no intention of doing anything of the sort. I only want to warn you against habits which may do mischief & which will certainly tend to make your own school days miserable. Society is like a looking-glass; if you smile at it, a smile is returned to you; if you look crossly at it, it returns an unkind look to you.

I love you intensely & wish for your happiness in every way, so I give you my best advice. Please regard all I have said as very kind words of love not as rebuke . . .

With a heart full of love

Try on dearie

I remain

Your ever loving father

E. Lamburn

ELIZABETH AIKEN (1832–1897)

grandmother

A great many of the letters in this collection were written by writers –
naturally, because a writer is already and permanently in writing mode.
But there are still some individuals who keep up an older tradition by
devoting a regular time each week to correspondence between family
and friends, and they become very good at it. Here is a grandmother
from a previous generation whose birthday letter to the little girl named
after her could serve as a model of the genre. At least three of her
descendants – Conrad, Jane and Joan – did become writers. This may
have been due to Elizabeth's husband, who was a friend of Ralph
Waldo Emerson, and minister of the First Congregational Church in
New Bedford, a fraternity rich in writers.

Cambridge [Mass]
May 19th, 1895

Dear Little Elizabeth,

When you get this letter you will be four years old! When you were three
years old, Grandma was with you, do you remember it? Now I am way off in
Cambridge and can't see any little 'kittens' so I have to write her a little letter
to tell her how I should like to see her to wish her a happy birthday, but it is
such a long, long way to Savannah over the big water that I can not come to
see her. So I will send a dollar for you to buy 'ice cream' for your supper and
take the rest of the money to buy something for you and Conrad to
remember grandma by. Papa and Mama will read this to you and will buy the
ice cream for you as you are not big enough yet. But if you are a real good
little girlie you will soon be as good as cousin Ruby is & then you can help
mama as she helps her mama. Now you have a new little baby brother that

Grandma has not seen. Does he laugh & crow when you play with him yet? Other little brother is big enough to run alone now I suppose so he can play with you and Conrad.

Now you must have a real nice time for your birthday & Grandma will remember it & think about you.

With much love & four
kisses for your four years
From your loving
Grandma
O. El. Aiken

ARTHUR PITT CHAMBERS CARY (1864–1937)

civil engineer

Arthur Cary, from an Anglo-Irish family, married Charlotte Joyce, a descendant of 'strange Mountainy men' with antique Welsh connections. Their elder son, to become a distinguished novelist, was named Joyce Cary. When he was nine his mother died, followed, when he was sixteen, by his stepmother, Dora. When Joyce heard the news he wrote immediately to his father. Then, very distressed and without telling anybody, he set out from school at Bristol for home in London. He was picked up at Paddington station and brought back. His father wrote

May 1905

My dear old boy,

I am sure that you are bitterly sorry, but you must not make me a greater burden than I already have.

Your letter was another blow to me for you know old boy there are times in this life when we must not give way no matter how we feel so my dear old boy you must be brave now and do your very best for my sake and the sake of dear Dora – We are going to take her to Rusthall Church tomorrow her Mother and Father are there –

Good bye for the present I know you will try to be brave for my sake. Work and play with all your might.

Ever your affectionate father

Arthur Cary

HELEN BEATRIX POTTER (1866–1943)

children's author and illustrator

Beatrix Potter's books and drawings are exceptionally delightful and thoroughly unsentimental. They have been popular all of this century. The first, *The Tale of Peter Rabbit*, appeared in letter form, written on 4 September 1893 to Noel Moore, whose mother had been Beatrix Potter's governess. It did not become a book for several years until the author published it at her own expense. Frederick Warne reprinted it to start their now world-famous edition, in 1902. Miss Potter became not only one of Warne's most profitable authors but a close friend of the family. She was engaged to Frederick's son Norman, but he died from pernicious anaemia, aged thirty-seven, so there was no wedding. Having dedicated *The Tale of Two Bad Mice* to Norman's niece, Winifred, Beatrix moved to the Lake Distract, married a solicitor and took up farming. She had no children. A collection of her many letters to the children of others was compiled by Judy Taylor in 1992. When asked by this editor to choose her favourite, she recommended this one. (Winifred also became a book illustrator.)

To Winifred Warne

September 6 '05
Gwaynyog
Nr Denbigh

My dear Winifred,

Would you like a letter from the 'Peter Rabbit Lady?' I want to tell you all about my 2 bunnies, I have got them with me here.

They are called Josey and Mopsy: Josey is a dear rabbit, she is so tame, although she is only a common wild one, who lived in a rabbit hole under a hedge. A boy caught her when she was quite a baby, she could sit in my hand. She is 3 years old now.

The other rabbit Mopsy is quite young, but it is frightened and silly; I am not quite sure whether I shall keep it; perhaps I shall take it into the wood and let it run away down a rabbit hole.

We picked such lots of mushrooms yesterday, my cousin and I and the gardener.

We looked out after breakfast and we saw a naughty old man with a basket, & a little girl with a black shawl <u>quite full</u> of mushrooms. So we ran out in a great hurry to get some before they were all stolen.

I am going to put a picture of mushrooms in a book. I have got my hedgehog here with me too; she enjoys going by train, she is always very hungry when she is on a journey. I carry her in a little basket and the bunnies in a small wooden box, I don't take any tickets for them.

My hedgehog Mrs. Tiggy-winkle is a great traveller, I don't know how many journeys she hasn't done.

The next journey will be quite a short one, I think I am going to the sea-side on Saturday.

I wonder if I shall find any crabs and shells and shrimps. Mrs. Tiggy-winkle won't eat shrimps; I think it is very silly of her, she will eat worms and beetles, and I am sure that shrimps would be much nicer. I think you must ask Mrs. Tiggy-winkle to tea when she comes back to London later on, she will drink milk like anything, out of a doll's tea-cup!

With a great many kisses from your
loving friend
Beatrix Potter.

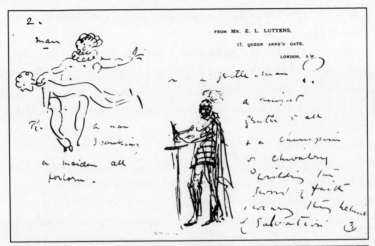

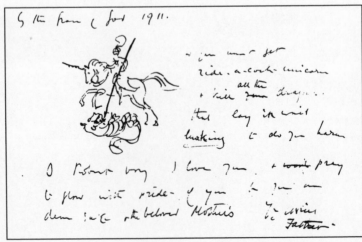

SIR EDWIN LANDSEER LUTYENS (1869–1944)

architect

Lutyens designed at all levels, from the massive Imperial-style Viceroy's House in New Delhi, through country houses, workers' cottages, the Cenotaph in Whitehall, down to tumblers and doorknobs.

Lutyens's father retired from the army to take up painting. He helped Sir Edwin Landseer with his lions in Trafalgar Square, hence the son's name. Young Lutyens fell rapturously in love with Lady Emily Lytton. They planned to live in a little white house in the country and do everything together. In fact they lived in huge Regency houses in London. When not absorbed in his work, he socialized; she was appallingly shy and stayed at home. He hated holidays; she relished a month by the sea with their five children. He loathed the sea and, rather than face it on his honeymoon, sat beside Emily on the beach but turned his deckchair round and faced the seaside architecture. At mealtimes they scarcely spoke; they read instead.

Emily met Annie Besant and was attracted to Theosophy and especially its young messiah, Krishnamurti, yet the marriage pursued its difficult course to a finally more kindly old age. But why had this apparently ill-matched couple not separated long before? *Why did they write to each other almost every day?*

Sir Edwin's letters to his children demonstrate that communication is more than punctuation and spelling. One to Robert, in 1906, commands, 'Give mother a great big hug & kiss for me & one thing – will you do it for me? Just give the back of your neck a kiss for me.' Another, given here in full, is characteristically illustrated.

21.11 [1911]
From Mr. E.L. Lutyens
17 Queen Anne's Gate
London S.W.

My darling Robert

Are you a unicorn – & parcel of groundsel – is it true that there are in you the makings of a man & a gentle man. Some times I wonder if the report of your being a unicorn is true. A unicorn (is thought by some) to be a noble beast – a beastie & [sacred?] heraldic at that and gets his point of horn into all sorts of places that it didn't ought.

[drawing]

Nannie for instance and other little girls. Or a parcel of groundsel only fit for canaries to peck at, or the makings of a man or a gentleman [drawing] a man spanking a maiden all forlorn [drawing of knight] a knight greater than all and a champion of chivalry wielding the sword of faith and wearing this helmet of salvation and giving the old devils one what-for – why not! [drawing] and don't think but do the right. I mean 'do' the wrong. You know what I mean.

Now when you feel rotten & cross just put your sword in your teeth & hold your shield over your head & do all you can to honour your mother & darling boy, do love her – in the same way as she loves you & let me know that should I have to go away to other worlds (things like this do happen) I shall feel and know that this is Robert and his good sword of faith to stand by help and protect her.

I wish all this to you as though you have grown up but I know really that you are only a little wee boy – but I am alone & by myself and feel lonely (Mr Lonely at 'ome – ask Ursula if you may read her letter & tho' you are only a little wee boy I like to think of the great many things little boys have done in the past & pray my little boy may do in the future – real great things that bring him to the precious fruits of all worlds. Now enjoy these fruits but never give them names. Tell mother that I have given Mrs Tyler 30/- on this the 21st day of August in the 2nd year of the reign of George V by the grace of God 1911. [drawing] and you must get ride-a-cock unicorn and kill all the dragons that lay in wait lurking to do you harm.

O Robert boy I love you and pray to glow with pride of you for your own dear sake and the beloved Mother's

Yr loving Father

P & O.S.N. Co.
S.S.
[Dec 1913]

My darlings own & 5.

What a splendid roll of names Barbara, Robert, Ursula, Elizabeth & Mary. Here I am on board S.S. 'Egypt' nearing Aden at the bottom of the red sea.

I dont mean quite what I have written – am still float – but on the southern end the bottom of the map.

What would you say today all bright hot hot sun – & a strong wind raking us from fore & aft which makes a climate the most delightful.

The boat is cram full of people It ought to be called the S S Sardinia as we are packed like sardines in our own juices. There are big men little men little men with big noses little men with little noses big men with little & big men with big noses. Every [illegible] & kind of hair.

Ladies ditto one in particular with a nose enormous & one poor old whisp of a thing that has lost her [bridge?] & could not if she would fiddle with it.

A few pale children & 2 little black ones for all the world like little shrimps that have been dipped in an ink pot. & there is a poor little horror of a thing most sad & pathetic. (I here stop to wipe my nose) a piebald one.

Fat men, thin men tall & short – with women kind to match in every sort of variety & mixed up various thin ones in concert last night & they all sang in the tops of their voices. If you listened to the swish swash of the waters you could not hear the song. If you listened to the singing you could not hear the sea – most of the people on board are box wallers. Ask Chippy what a box waller is – it means a merchant & waller is a fellow. & a box suggests grocery – soft & hard ware & anythingdone up in bales which men buy firm & sell to each other.

I address them & you Barbie daughter own for you to read it to your sisters & brother & when you have read it you can cut it up in 5 pieces & you can each have one.

Give my love to memsahib nannie & a huge 5 volumed packet of love to memsahib mother – & just smother her with care love & kisses – & do all this for me in my name.

Ever your 5 hearted
        Father who loves his bairns to absolute distraction.
God bless you darlings & make happy good – altogether happy.

RUDYARD KIPLING (1865–1936)

writer

Rudyard Kipling was born in India, where his father taught in the Art School of Bombay. Aged six, his blissfully happy life was upturned when he was sent home to England to lodge with a couple in Southsea. The story *Baa Baa Black Sheep* reflects the unhappy years spent with them; *Stalky & Co.* is based on his later life at school. At seventeen he rejoined his parents in Lahore and commenced a swiftly successful career as journalist and author. He married his American agent's sister and they had three children, Josephine (1893), Elsie (1896) and John (1897).

Literary awards did not mean very much to Kipling. But receiving a degree from Oxford University made a good subject for a letter to John, then aged ten.

13 Norham Gardens
Oxford
Thursday. June 27 1907

My dear John:

I was very glad to hear from Mrs. Clarke that you seem to have been behaving yourself decently: but I don't think much of the postcards you send. They are short and small. However, in a few days I myself will be able to get your news at first hand.

Sorry about the weather. It has been most disgusting in our parts of the world too and coming down from Durham on Tuesday afternoon it was Unusual Vile. Yesterday was dark, windy and warm. We went down to Oxford by an early train which reached there at 10.30. On the platform a man met me with my scarlet and grey gown. It's rather like an African parrot. Then we drove in a carriage till I came to a wonderful hall – a sort of

baronial hall. Mummy went away with Mrs. Osler and I was left among a
crowd of men all in gowns of all colours – red, black and grey. I knew a lot
of the men, and a butler handed round biscuits and wines. Presently we
formed a procession – two by two – and were put into order like boys at
school. Then we all walked out into the streets and for 20 minutes we
'ceased not to advance in our stately procession' through the streets. They
were crowded with people and all the people cheered Mark Twain who
walked in front of me. And when they weren't cheering and shouting you
could hear the Kodak shutters click-clicking like gun locks. That was great
fun. Then we were walked through wonderful quadrangles and halls and
archways into another and most enormous baronial hall with marvellous
windows and there we were told to wait till we were asked for. We sat about
on old oak benches and waited – and waited – and waited. Every now and
then a splendid person in a gown would come in and lead away several of
us, along a great stone passage into the shadow of a dark doorway and then
we who were left behind heard the roars of applause and shouting from a
multitude in the distance – exactly like prisoners on a desert island hearing
savages eating their companions. That was very fine. If we looked along the
stone passage into the dark hall we could just see a figure all in gold, like a
Burmese idol, sitting high on a throne. That was the Chancellor of the
University in his robes of office, sitting on his stately seat, ready to welcome
the men who were getting their degrees. And we waited, *and* we waited,
AND we waited and talked to each other. At last a man I knew at the Club
said: – 'D'you think we can smoke?' and a fine person in a gown said: – 'Not
here! You can smoke under that archway.' So we went out and Mark Twain
came with us and three or four other men followed and we had a smoke like
naughty little boys, under a big archway.

Last of all – about 12.30 we were sent for – in a batch of seven. When I
say 'we' I mean me and the men who were getting my particular sort of
degree.

We came into a huge round hall, packed with people up to the ceiling. I
looked about and saw Mummy looking very sweet and beautiful and then I
didn't mind. All the young undergraduates sat in the gallery and shouted
remarks. A very old man, with a small voice, made a speech in Latin about
each of us and the boys shouted to him to speak up. When he couldn't one
boy said: – 'Hush! You'll wake the baby!' And another said: – ''Tisn't polite
to whisper in public.' And another said: – 'Try Mother Siegel's Syrup.' When
Mark Twain went up they shouted like anything and they cheered and they

asked him nice questions. I was the last of the lot and the man who spoke about me in Latin was very tired and he could not be heard, even by me. Then one of the undergraduates said in a nice confidential voice: – 'You'll tell us about it afterwards Rudyard.' Then the Chancellor shook hands with me and said a nice thing in Latin and then all the boys sang: 'He's a jolly good fellow!' And so I was made a Doctor of Letters.

While we were waiting I met an old school-master of mine who had been my French master and while he was talking to me I was introduced to a great French musician, a Monsieur Saint-Saëns, and I talked to him, no end – in French! I was awfully proud of that. Then I saw my own dear Headmaster, Cormell Price, and a lot of people I knew and when we all came out of the hall to go to lunch who should I meet but the Pater! He'd seen all the ceremony and wasn't a bit tired. Then we lunched in a wonderful room, and then I went to a garden party and then I went out to dinner. Mummy wore her blue silk dress and looked simply *lovely*. I had to wear my gown at the garden party and I felt as if I'd forgotten our bath-sponge on the way to the bath aboard ship. Gowns are funny things. They flop about one's legs.

You can imagine I was *very* tired. Mummy stayed here, in this delightful house and went to bed early. She is resting to-day but we want to go to see the Oxford Pageant this afternoon. Then to-morrow we come home and I think on Saturday you'll see me coming along to haul you out of Rottingdean by the slack of your breeches! Hurrah! I hear all you pug-dogs are having high old times and that you went over and played in our piece of land. Glad you got the key. Give my love to Larry and my specialest and most particular thanks to Mrs. Clarke for writing to us so fully about things.

Perhaps some day we'll get some summer weather. Meantime I am
Your affectionate

Dad

Mount Stephen House
Field, B.C. Canada
October 12 1907

Dear Sir – My esteemed Son – O John, etc.

We reached this place last night and found your first letter from school waiting for us. It had been sent on from Montreal. You can just imagine how delighted we were to get it and how we read it over and over again.

I am very pleased to know that you like school – I feel sure that you will like it more and more as time goes on and you settle down and make your own friends. But I know exactly how homesick you feel at first. I can remember how I felt when I first went to school at Westward Ho!. But my school was more than two hundred miles from my home – my Father and Mother were in India and I knew that I should not see them for years. The school was more than two hundred boys of all ages from eighteen to twelve. I was nearly the youngest – and the grub was simply beastly.

Now with you, you are not thirty miles from home – you are by no means the youngest chap there – and they look after you in a way that no one dreamed of doing when I was young. Likewise you have the pull of living in the village where you were born, full of all the people you have known all your life with Auntie Georgie round the corner . . .

I am rather pleased with you about one thing. You know I never mind jumping on you when you have done something I don't like – the same way I generally tell you when you have behaved decently. Well from all I can discover, you behaved yourself like a man when you felt homesick. I understand that you did not flop about and blub and whine but carried on quietly. *Good Man!* Next time it will come easier to you to keep control over yourself and the time after that easier still . . .

> Bateman's
> Burwash
> Sussex
> June 9, 1908

Dear Bird [Elsie],

The house is four times emptier and five times larger than it was at 11 o'clock this morning. Can it be possible, said Mr. Campbell, that the departure of a F-t P-rs-n in a pony-cart has had anything to do with this surprising change? I think so.

This afternoon after lunch I nobly weeded the peony bed under the wall with a knife. I am indeed an energetic worker. I was getting on splendidly till Mummy came out and helped me with a spud. Then we quarrelled and fought about our different systems of weeding. Mine was the Delicate and Refined (how like *me!*) Hers was the Careless and Slap-dash (how like you!) Anyway between us we weeded the peony bed.

After tea I went out with my Papa up to the village to enquire after

Colonel Feilden. He is a great deal better – has slept during the day and his breathing is easier. Aren't you glad? As my Papa and I walked up the footpath that leads to Ten Oak Shaw we saw a she-child about two foot high and a he-baby about eighteen inches high climb over the stile. There were a lot of cows in the meadow. The cows were naturally interested in the small things and that made 'em afraid. They stopped, hand in hand, and moved by little rushes at a time. Naturally the cows were more interested. Equally naturally the babes got more frightened. Though I had no daughter to protect me against the fierce onslaughts of the cows (they gurgled in their throats) I advanced alone to those small panic-stricken babes and escorted them past the ferocious cows, several of which whisked their tails. As soon as they got to the other side the kids scuttled over like rabbits. This is a tale of noble heroism!

There isn't any other news so I send you a few simple rules for Life in London.

1. Wash early and often with soap and hot water.
2. Do not roll on the grass of the parks. It will come off black on your dress.
3. Never eat penny buns, oysters, periwinkles or peppermints on the top of a bus. It annoys the passengers.
4. Be kind to policemen. You never know when you may be taken up.
5. Never stop a motor bus with your foot. It is not a croquet ball.
6. Do not attempt to take pictures off the wall of the National Gallery or to remove cases of butterflies from the Natural History Museum. You will be noticed if you do.
7. Avoid late hours, pickled salmon, public meetings, crowded crossings, gutters, water-carts and over-eating.

That is all I can think of at present: but if you ever feel doubtful about your conduct, you have only to write and I myself will instruct you further, said Mr. Campbell.

Dear love from us both.

Ever your

Daddo

Bateman's,
Burwash,
Sussex.
July 29 1908

My dear Miss Kipling,

Your Little Brother returned from school yesterday. I repaired to
Rottingdean in the Motor via Brighton stopping at the Queen of Watering
Places to pay a pleasant and instructive visit to a Dentist of my acquaintance
who kindly walked round my Beaming Smile with spanners, wrenches,
thumbscrews and similar pleasant tools.

At 3.30 p.m. I reached Master Kipling's seminary and found your Poor
Brother dissolved in tears at the thought of

His new "straw hat".

parting with his Dearly Loved Companions, his affectionate Matron and his
Respected Head Master. When his sobs had abated somewhat, he flung
himself at Mrs Stanford's feet and pleaded most eloquently to be allowed to
Remain and pursue his studies – if necessary on Bread and Water! Such
were his simple words. I carried him, still weeping, to the house of Lady
Burne-Jones where at 4.15 p.m. he made a Delicate Tea of not more than
six or seven slices of Bread and Butter, several hot tea-cakes and a few
pounds of chocolate cake. At 5 he consented to get into the motor and with
many a regretful glance at St Aubyns (the home of so many pleasant

Reminiscences) I carried him away, the prey of uncontrollable emotion.
Seldom have I seen one so young so loath to revisit his Ancestral home. He
complained that no time would now be allowed him to continue his studies

in Latin and Mathematics – the objects of his deepest interest. He further stated that his sister was a Slacker and at Lewes (his sobs being less frequent) staggered to the Post Office to send her a telegram to this effect.

(The true version)

The young imp sang nearly all the way home and struck up "The church's one foundation" at the head of Lewes High Street! I had to remind him it wasn't the Heathfield road! When we got home he ran about till he got the bat and stumps and made me bowl to him. He sat up to dinner at 7.30 and went to bed at 8.30 about as blissfully happy a young mortal as I've ever seen. He is now (9 a.m.) rampaging round my room, after having washed out my old stilo, wondering what he shall do next. I foresee my days will be evil and hectic till you come back. I am trying to get him to send you a few lines but he shies off the subject. He has all his exam papers with him which he wants Miss Blaikie to look at.

Now he has hauled up a chair to my table and says he will write to you. Oh Lor! Don't you *ever* be a father, my Bird. He's shaking my table like an earthquake!

With love,
Dad.

P.S. I think he wants being kicked with love and forethought.

Kipling, who loved being a father, suffered the death of Josephine from pneumonia, aged not quite seven, and of John. Owing to poor eyesight, John was not accepted for active service in World War I. But his father, who was publicly promoting recruitment, used his influence and John was commissioned in the Irish Guards on his eighteenth birthday. Six weeks later he was killed at the Battle of Loos.

KENNETH GRAHAME (1859–1932)

writer

Kenneth and Elspeth Grahame had only one child, Alastair. Every night his father told the little boy a never-ending story about a Mr Toad, a Mr Badger, a Mr Rat, a Mr Mole and others. In 1907, Alastair, aged four, was sent to Littlehampton with his governess on a seven-week holiday, during which Grahame wrote him fifteen letters. Fortunately, the governess preserved them. They set down in outline the saga of the bedtime story characters and were, in effect, the first draft of *The Wind in the Willows*. Here is the first of those letters.

11 Durham Villas
London
10 May 1907

My darling Mouse [Alastair's nickname],

This is a birthday letter to wish you very many happy returns of the day. I wish we could have been all together, but we shall meet again soon and then we will have <u>treats</u>. I have sent you two picturebooks, one about Brer Rabbit, from Daddy, and one about some other animals, from Mummy. And we have sent you a boat, painted red, with mast and sails to sail in the round pond by the windmill – and Mummy has sent you a boat-hook to catch it when it comes ashore. Also Mummy has sent you some sand-toys to play in the sand with, and a card game. Have you heard about the Toad? He was never taken prisoner by brigands at all. It was all a horrid low trick of his. He wrote that letter himself – the letter saying that a hundred pounds must be put in the hollow tree. And he got out of the window early one morning and went off to a town called Buggleton and went to the Red Lion Hotel and there he found a party that had just motored down from London and while they were having breakfast he went into the stable-yard and found their motor-car and went off in it without even saying Poop-poop! And now he has vanished and everyone is looking for him, including the police. I fear he is a bad low animal.

    Good-bye, from

your Daddy

CLAUDE DEBUSSY (1862–1918)

composer, pianist

Owing to his innovative style, involving the creation of sound pictures, Debussy became known as 'a musical impressionist', a term he detested. *Images*, *La Mer* and *Prélude à l'après-midi d'un Faune* are amongst his best-known works. In 1908 he married Emma Bardac (his second wife); they already had a daughter, Chouchou, who was born in 1905. She was five when she received the first 'letter' below, actually a series of six postcards of which the fourth has been lost. 'Outre Croche' is a reference to Debussy's alter ego, Monsieur Croche, and to *Mémoires d'outre-tombe*, the autobiography of the writer and statesman François-René, Vicomte de Chateaubriand, 1768–1848.

Vienna
2 December 1910

The memoirs of 'outre Croche'
1. Once there was a papa who lived in exile . . . 2. and every day he missed his little Chouchou. 3. The inhabitants of the city saw him walking past and murmured 'Why does that gentleman look so sad in our gay and beautiful city?' [. . .] 5. So Chouchou's papa went into a shop run by an old, very ugly man and his even uglier daughter, he politely removed his hat and using deaf-mute gestures asked for the most beautiful postcards they had, so that he could write to his darling little daughter . . . The ugly old man was very moved by this and as for his daughter, she died on the spot! 6. The said papa went back to his hotel, wrote this story which would make a goldfish weep, and put all his love into the signature below, which is his greatest claim to fame.
LepapadeChouchou

In the second letter, Chouchou is eight. Xantho is the family's dog.

St. Petersburg
Grand Hotel d'Europe
11 December 1913

Ma chère petite Chouchou,

Your poor papa is very late replying to your nice little letter. But you mustn't be cross with him . . . He's very sad not to have seen your pretty face for so long or heard you singing or shouting with laughter, in short all the noise which sometimes makes you an unbearable little girl, but more often a charming one.

How is that genius M. Czerny getting on? Do you know:

the 'air de ballet' for fleas?

And old Xantho? Is he still being good? Is he still digging up the garden? You have my permission to give him a thorough scolding!

At the Koussevitsky's house in Moscow there are two lovely bulldogs with eyes like the frog in the salon (we're great friends, I think you'd like them) and a bird which sings almost as well as Miss Teyte.

It's all very nice but don't imagine I can forget you; even for a second. Far from it, the only thing I think about is when I'm going to see you again. Until then, love and lots of kisses from your old papa.

C.D.

Be very nice to your poor mama; do all you can to see she doesn't get too worried!

VICTORIA, MARCHIONESS OF MILFORD HAVEN
(1863–1950)

Princess Victoria of Hesse was Queen Victoria's favourite grand-daughter. They had in common a strong sense of family responsibility. The princess married Prince Louis of Battenburg whose name was tact-fully anglicized during World War I to Mountbatten. In 1884, Louis wrote to the future King George V, Victoria 'is such a lovely darling girl ... and I am nearly off my head altogether with feeling so jolly'. The marriage was a happy one; they had four children, the youngest of whom was Lord Louis Mountbatten, born in 1900. He served in the Royal Navy for much of his life and became the last viceroy of India. An IRA bomb planted on his yacht in Ireland ended his life.

Princess Victoria wrote this letter to Louis when he was about six. A nickname was *de rigueur* in spite of his having a string of official Christian names. Queen Victoria suggested Nickie but there were so many Russian Nickies in the family that this one became Dick, or Dickie.

This letter dated 8 May 1911 was sent to Dickie at Locker's Park School near Berkhamsted in Hertfordshire.

❖

87 Queen's Gate,
S.W.
8th May 1911

My dear Dick,

Thank you so much for your nice letter, I am so glad you find the work in B.II not so difficult as you feared. I agree in thinking the master was unfair to you, & that his excuse afterwards was not quite truthful probably, but you must not forget that masters are only ordinary human beings & that this one has evidently a nasty temper; when his anger had passed you see he did not demand the *fine* (not find as you write it), so he probably felt he had been unfair himself & repented of it. It would have been better if he had said so, instead of giving you a fancy explanation but the mistaken pride of a grown person towards a boy prevented him. Do not judge him too hardly for his fault & bear him malice for it. That he is a person you & the others can not like is natural. Only don't nurse your dislike, for that would be unfair.

I hope you will like your cold baths, if you feel warm after rubbing down afterwards, they are sure to be good for you. Only if you feel chilly afterwards it is better to give them up.

Papa comes up this afternoon to go to a dinner & ball with Louise and me & to-morrow evening we go to 'Court' in Buckingham Palace. The whole family were at Windsor for a service on the anniversary of Uncle Bertie's death & we arranged with cousin George that you should see the Coronation procession start & return, at the Palace.

Much love from all.

Ever your loving Mama

June 26 1946

KEN WOOD,
HAMPSTEAD,
LONDON, N.W.

My dear Dickie,

That was a lovely birthday surprise you gave us yesterday when you telegraphed the result of your passing out exam. We are so proud & pleased that you have done so very well.

First at Keyham and Ninth all together is better than we ever thought you could be & I am sure you must be delighted.

That both of our boys have worked & done so well as naval cadets makes us very happy, for it is not only the actual places you have taken in your final tests we are thinking of, but more even that both Georgie & you have never given us a moment's worry by your general life & conduct as cadets – for after all, to do well at one's work may be due a great deal to the natural gifts one has been born with, but to come through the many temptations that assail a boy in his school life so well as you have done, is a sign of a good character, & that is your own doing, therefore a better thing in our eyes than the highest place in exams. I have seen, my dear child, how steadily you have struggled against your faults, and with what good success & I know how difficult such a struggle is, for many of your faults are mine, too. The 'black pig' who when you were a little fellow would at times look nearly as big as yourself, has remained a little starved object, whilst you have grown, & your good qualities have developed, & this has made me more happy than you can perhaps quite understand.

Now your school life is near its end, & the bigger, more responsible life of an office in the Service is beginning, may God help & strengthen you my very dear boy, & never forget that we love you very dearly and have been young ourselves once, & shall be able to understand the difficulties outside & in yourself which you may meet in your new life, and if we can help by word or deed will always do so.

JACK LONDON (1876–1916)

writer

Jack London was born in San Francisco, the illegitimate son of two astrologers. His father never acknowledged responsibility, his mother cared little for him. He took refuge in alcohol and searched for an ideal life companion who would be as adventurous, forthright and unconventional as himself. He abandoned his first wife and two daughters for a second who was adventurous but simple-minded. Farmer as well as writer, he had great sympathy for his employees but allowed them to cheat him, which no doubt led to the dismal state of his finances, implicit in this letter to his thirteen-year-old daughter Joan. Joan grew up to write his biography, more in sorrow than in anger, thereby exhibiting a forgiving nature. London ended his life in agony twenty-four hours after taking lethal doses of two drugs that counteracted each other, causing a lingering death.

February 24, 1914

Dear Joan: –

In reply to yours of February 10, 1914. I have just got back from the East, and am taking hold of my business. Please find herewith check for $4.50, according to account presented by you. When I tell you that this leaves me a balance in the bank of $3.46, you will understand how thin the ice is upon which I am skating.

I note by your letter that you have been charging schoolbooks in my account at Smith's. Never again do a thing like this. Never be guilty of charging to anybody's account when you have not received permission from that person to charge to their account. I shall make a point of sending you

the money for your schoolbooks when you write to me for same, or, if I
have not the money, of giving you permission to charge to my account. If I
am away, and if Mrs. Eliza Shepard has not the money, she may also give
you permission to charge to my account. Under no other circumstances
except those of permission, may you in the future charge anything to any
account of mine anywhere. This is only clean, straight, simple business,
Joan.

Now I have what most persons would deem a difficult letter to write; but
I have always found that by being frank and true, no thing is difficult to say.
All one has to say is all that he feels or thinks.

Let me tell you a little something about myself: All my life has been
marked by what, in lack of any other term, I must call 'disgust'. When I
grow tired or disinterested in anything, I experience a disgust which settles
for me that thing forever. I turn the page down there and then. When a colt
on the ranch, early in its training, shows that it is a kicker or a bucker or a
bolter or a balker, I try patiently and for a long time to remove, by my
training, such deleterious traits; and then at the end of a long time if I find
that these vicious traits continue, suddenly there comes to me a disgust, and
I say Let the colt go. Kill it, sell it, give it away. So far as I am concerned I
am finished with the colt. So it has been with all things in my whole life
from the very first time that I can remember anything of myself. I have
been infatuated with many things, I have worked through many things, have
become disgusted with those many things. Please believe me, – and have
turned down the pages forever and irrevocably on those many things. I am
not stating to you my strength, but my weakness. These colossal disgusts
that compel me to turn pages are weaknesses of mine, and I know them;
but they are there. They are part of me. I am so made.

Years ago I warned your mother that if I were denied the opportunity of
forming you, sooner or later I would grow disinterested in you, I would
develop a disgust, and that I would turn down the page. Of course, your
mother, who is deaf to all things spiritual, and appreciative, and
understanding, smiled to herself and discounted what I told her. Your
mother today understands me no more than has she ever understood me –
which is no understanding at all.

Now, do not make the mistake of thinking that I am now running away
from all filial duties and responsibilities. I am not. I shall take care of you; I
shall take care of Baby B., I shall take care of your mother. I shall take care
of the three of you. You shall have food and shelter always. But,

unfortunately, I have turned the page down, and I shall be no longer interested in the three of you.

I do not imagine that I shall ever care to send you to the University of California, unless you should develop some tremendous desire to do specific things in the world that only a course in the University of California will fit you for. I certainly shall never send you to the University of California in recognition of the bourgeois valuation put upon the University pigskin.

I should like to see you marry for love when you grow up. That way lies the best and sweetest of human happiness. On the other hand, if you want career instead, I'll help you to pursue whatever career you elect. When you were small, I fought for years the idea of your going on the stage. I now withdraw my opposition. If you desire the stage with its consequent (from my point of view) falseness, artificiality, sterility and unhappiness, why go ahead, and I will do what I can to help you to it.

But please, please remember that in whatever you do from now on, I am uninterested. I desire to know neither your failures nor your successes; wherefore please no more tell me of your markings in High School, and no longer send me your compositions.

When you want money, within reason, I shall send it to you if I have it. Under any and all circumstances, so long as I live, you shall receive from me food in your stomach, a roof that does not leak, warm blankets, and clothing to cover you.

A year from now I expect to have a little money. At the present moment, if I died, I should die One hundred thousand dollars in debt. Therefore, a year from now I may be more easy with you in money matters than I am capable of being now.

I should like to say a few words further about the pages I turn down because of the disgusts that come upon me. I was ever a lover of fatherhood. I loved fatherhood over love of woman. I have been jealous of my seed, and I have never wantonly scattered my seed. I gave you, well (we'll say my share at least) a good body and a good brain. I had a father's fondest love and hope for you. But you know, in bringing up colts, colts may be brought up good and bad, all according to the horseman who brings up the colts. You were a colt. Time and fate and mischance, and a stupid mother, prevented me from having a guiding hand in your upbringing. I waited until you, who can dramatize 'Sohrab and Rustum' could say for yourself what you wanted. Alas, as the colt, you were already ruined by your trainer. You

were lied to, you were cheated. I am sorry; it was not your fault. But when
the time for you to decide (not absolutely between your mother and me) –
to decide whether or not I might have a little hand in showing and training
you to your paces in the big world, you were already so ruined by your
trainer, that you declined. It is not your fault. You were trained. It is not your
mother's fault – she was born stupid, stupid she will live, and stupid she will
die. It was nobody's fault – except God's fault, if you belive in God. It is a
sad mischance, that is all. In connection therewith I can only quote to you
Kipling's 'Toolungala Stockyard Chorus':

'And some are sulky, while some will plunge.
  (*So ho! Steady! Stand still, you!*)
Some you must gentle, and some you must lunge.
  (*There! There! Who wants to kill you?*)

Some – there are losses in every trade –
Will break their hearts ere bitted and made,
Will fight like fiends as the rope cuts hard,
And die dumb-mad in the breaking-yard.'

Whether or not you may die dumb-mad, I know not, I do know that you
have shown, up to the present time, only docility to your trainer. You may
cheat and fool your trainer, and be ruined by your trainer. I only think that I
know that you are too much of a diplomat to die over anything – result of
your reaction over your training, plus your inherent impulse to avoid
trouble, kick-up, and smashing of carts and harnesses.

You cannot realize all this letter. You may when you are older. Save it for
that time. But I have lost too many colts not to be philosophical in losing
you. It might be thought that I am unfair to your youthfulness – yet you
dramatized 'Sohrab and Rustum,' and calmly state to me narrow-minded,
bourgeois prejudices (instilled into your mind by your mother), such as: My
present wife, my Love Woman, is all that is awful and horrible in that I do
truly love her, and in that she does truly love me.

All my life I have been overcome by disgust, which has led me to turn
pages down, and those pages have been turned down forever. It is my
weakness, as I said before. Unless I should accidentally meet you on the
street, I doubt if I shall ever see you again. If you should be dying, and
should ask for me at your bedside, I should surely come; on the other hand,
if I were dying I should not care to have you at any bedside. A ruined colt is

a ruined colt, and I do not like ruined colts.

Please let me know that you have read this letter in its entirety. You will not understand it entirely. Not for years, and perhaps never, will you understand. But, being a colt breaker, I realize that a colt is ruined by poor training, even though the colt never so realizes.

Whenever you want money, within reason, for clothes, books, spending, etc., write me for it, and if I have it at the time, I shall send it to you.

Jack London

In fact, this was not the last letter Joan received from her father. One supposes that she accepted it as the explanation it was intended to be and not as the excuse it could have been seen as.

LETTERS FROM THE FIRST WORLD WAR

(1914–1918)

All the letters in this section were written by men on active service to their own or other people's children.

FRANK HEATH sent this picture letter to his eldest daughter, Aileen. He lived in Cornwall, working with a group called the Lamorna artists. He enlisted as a volunteer in Lady Cunliffe Lister's 2nd Sportsmans Battalion of the Artists' Rifles (Royal Fusiliers). After training at Hare Hall, Romford, he was posted to France in spring 1915. His reaction to the German chlorine gas was so violent – it gave him meningitis – that his wife came to France with a doctor to fetch him home, and he was invalided out of the army. Transcribed, the letter reads:

Aileen –   Hare Hall (rabbit & house)

Love from Daddy. These pretty pictures are where he is staying – Grandmama will read you this letter.
[Drawing] Daddy as a soldier – are there any pretty [flower drawing] in your garden yet? and do you water them? [drawing] [drawing of beds] This is how daddy goes to bed – he has got such a nice cot & has to make it himself every morning – Mummy is at the sea, a long way away & will soon come back and see you – [drawing of Mummy]. How is Cockerell Ginger & Black Bunny & Tiny Mouse?

Good bye little girl
Your loving Daddy
[picture of cow] MOO COW

Hare Hall

Aileen -

Love from Daddy. These pretty pictures are where he is staying. Grand m'am will read you this letter. Daddy as a Soldier. Are there any pretty [flowers] in your garden yet? and do you water them.

This is how daddy goes to bed - he has got such a nice cot & has to made it himself every morning. Mummy is at the sea, a long way away & will soon come back and see you. - How is Cockerell Ginger & Black Bunny & Tiny mouse - Good bye little girl. Your loving Daddy -

Moo Cow -

WILLIAM LEWIS BRITTON was also an artist. A Londoner, who served before the war with the 13th Hussars in India, he won prizes at water-colour exhibitions in Simla, India. In the Great War he was a private in Mechanical Transport and was mentioned in despatches on 29 November 1917. He drove a motor fire engine in Salonika, Greece, when that city burnt for ten days. Two enormous portfolios of Mr Britton's letters, with their witty illustrations, may be seen at the Imperial War Museum.

24th Oct 1917

My Dear Billie

Many thanks for your letter which came with Mamma's quite safely. I would like very much to send you something for your Birthday but I cannot buy any things for little boys here in Salonika. When I come home I will bring you something but now there are no shops since the fire when all the houses got burnt. Tell Mamma she must buy you something for me. I hope you like these pictures of the black pussy cat, I will do you a lot more, you must write and tell me how you like them. We are getting a lot of rain out here and we can see the snow on the top of the Mountains. I expect you will be getting bad weather now. You must be a good boy. I shall be home soon. Then we will have fine times again. Tell Mamma I have had a lot of letters and papers from her. Lots of Love & Kisses to you from

your Loving
Daddy
X X X X X

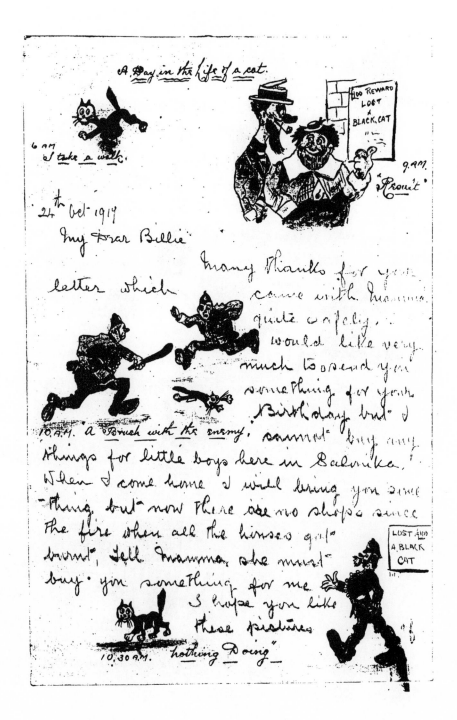

the black pussy cat, i will do you a lot more, you must write and tell me how you like them. we are getting a lot of rain out here and we can see the snow on the tops of the mountains. i expect you will be getting bad weather now. you must be a good boy. i shall

"at close quarters" 11.45

"a narrow shave" 1.0 P.M.

be brave again so we will have fine times again

12 Noon "now how have the mighty fallen"

2.0 P.M.

"Dinner" and papa's lots of love + kisses

tell mamma i got 31 letters

to you from your loving Daddie

4.30 "Home"

"'tis the end of a peaceful day"

My dear Billie

I think you look very nice in your photo and I am pleased to see you are growing such a big boy & hope you are quite well as I am. Good-night

Lots of Love and kisses from

'Where's the fire?' your loving

Daddy

x x x x

❖

FRANK FIELDER. This very sad but dignified letter is preserved in the Imperial War Museum and nothing is known about the writer other than that he was serving in France.

YMCA
On Active Service
With the British
Expeditionary Force
Wednesday April 23rd

Dear little girl,

Perhaps you will be very surprised to have a letter from France, and from me, but I am bound to write you a little letter to thank you very much indeed for the nice scarf you so kindly knitted for a soldier, and I am the lucky soldier who owns it now.

Of course, you perhaps made that scarf months and months ago when it was very cold, but it has only just been handed to me as a gift, the cold weather has almost finished now, in any case it is not cold enough to wear a scarf but I will keep it for ever, and take it to my home in London, when I go home for good, as a souvenir from you, although I have never seen you. I appreciate it very much indeed, thank you again.

If you would be so kind as to write me a little letter here is my address: –
925743. Driver Frank Fielder, 30th D.A.C. R.F.A. B.E.F.

From your unknown
soldier friend
Frank Fielder

P.S. My best wishes to all your family.

JAMES BELL FOULIS. A captain in the 5th Cameron Highlanders, who was born in 1883, James Bell Foulis is writing to his niece Nancy Lilburn in Renfrewshire from the Western Front.

Captain Foulis wrote a series of remarkable letters to his young niece. He speaks of the 'things' which make up his life, but gaily, so that the telling is possible to one so young. Her parents no doubt understood, and she would, later.

From another, undated letter to Nancy:
'Please write me another letter very very soon and tell me
all about school and dancing and parties and things . . .'

Captain Foulis was killed on the Somme;
he has no known grave.

B Coy, 5th Camerons
B.E.F.
13/10/15

My dear little Nancy,

I have now got over here and am living in a trench close to the Germans. It is rather a jolly trench for there are all sorts of little houses and snug little holes and corners dug out everywhere. Some of these little houses we use for sleeping in and others for our meals.

The 'Germis' are about 100 yards away, and we often throw shells and bombs and things at each other, but our trench is a jolly strong one so they cannot do us any harm.

We have got a lot of enormous rats and tiny mice. They scuttle and scamper about everywhere and do not bother about the war at all. This morning one of our soldiers killed a large rat with a spade. Now we have a bomb throwing machine, so we put this rat on to the machine and threw it all the way into the German trench. I wonder if they had it for breakfast!

It is rather pretty at night here there are so many wonderful lights in the sky. You see the flashing of big guns and of bursting shells very often but mostly a long way off. Then there are the rockets which are sent up every few minutes both by ourselves and the Germans. They light the sky almost like daylight, so that you can see every blade of grass in the ground between us and the Boches. They are fine to watch.

Now I hope you and Jimmy will write me a nice long letter and tell me all the funny things that have happened.

Heaps of love to yourself and Jimmy and Willie and everybody,

from
Uncle Jim

B.E.F./Saturday

My dear wee Nancy,

I am back in the trenches again and am going to write you a little letter to tell you about things.

We are living in a lovely big green wood and you would be surprised at the number of birds and things there are in it. They don't seem to care a button for all the shells that are flying about and keep on singing merrily all the time. There are cuckoos and turtle-doves, blackbirds and thrushes, robins linnets and all sorts of others, and even one or two pheasants.

There are also lots of great big frogs on the pools and they go croaking and chattering to themselves all day long.

We have got some carrier pigeons, which live in a dug out all for themselves. They are to carry messages for us in case the telephone wires get broken. When the Germans send over poisonous gas the pigeons are put into a bag so that they will not be killed by the gas.

There are a terrible lot of rats and mice in the trenches. They go scurrying about everywhere.

An officer has brought a ferret up today to kill some, – but I am afraid the ferret will soon get lost.

Heaps of love to you and Jim and Willie.

From

Uncle Jim

WALTER HINES PAGE (1855–1918)

American diplomat, ambassador to England during World War I

This letter to Walter Hines Page's grandson, Walter H. Page, Jr, was first published in *The Life and Letters of Walter H. Page*. Later on it was printed separately.

London, Christmas, 1915

<u>Sir,</u>

For your first Christmas, I have the honour to send you my most affectionate greetings; and in wishing you all good health, I take the liberty humbly to indicate some of the favours of fortune that I am pleased to think I enjoy in common with you.

<u>First</u> – I hear with pleasure that you are quite well content with yourself – not because of a reasoned conviction of your own worth, which would be mere vanity, and unworthy of you, but by reason of a philosophical disposition. It is too early for you to bother over problems of self-improvement – as for me it is too late; wherefore we are alike in the calm of our self-content. What others may think or say about us is a subject of the smallest concern to us. Therefore they generally speak well of us; for there is little satisfaction in speaking ill of men who care nothing for your opinion of them. Then, too, we are content to be where we happen to be – a fact that we did not order in the beginning and need not now concern ourselves about. Consider the eternal coming and going of folk. On every road many are travelling one way and an equal number are travelling the other way. It is obvious that, if they were all content to remain at the places whence they set forth, the distribution of the population would be the same. Why therefore move hither and yon at the cost of so much time and labour and money,

since nothing is accomplished thereby? We spare ourselves by being content to remain where we are. We thereby have the more time for reflection. Nor can we help observing with a smile that all persons who have good reason to see us themselves make the necessary journey after they discover that we are fixed.

Again, people about us are continually doing this service and that for some other people – running errands, mending fences, bearing messages, building, and tearing down; and they all demand equal service in return. Thus a large part of mankind keeps itself in constant motion like bubbles of water racing around a pool at the foot of a waterfall – or like rabbits hurrying into their warrens and immediately hurrying out again. Whereas, while these antics amuse and sadden us, we for the most part remain where we are. Hence our wants are few; they are generally most courteously supplied without our asking; or, if we happen to be momentarily forgotten, we can quickly secure anything in the neighbourhood by a little judicious squalling. Why, then, should we swirl as bubbles or scurry as rabbits? Our conquering self-possession gives a masterful charm to life that the victims of perpetual locomotion never seem to attain.

You have discovered, and my experience confirms yours, that a perpetual self-consciousness brings most of the misery of the world. Men see others who are richer than they; or more famous, or more fortunate – so they think; and they become envious. You have not reached the period of such empty vanity, and I have long passed it. Let us, therefore, make our mutual vows not to be disturbed by the good luck or the good graces of others, but to continue, instead, to contemplate the contented cat on the rug and the unenvious sky that hangs over all alike.

This mood will continue to keep our lives simple. Consider our diet. Could anything be simpler or better? We are not even tempted by the poisonous victuals wherewith mankind destroys itself. The very first sound law of life is to look to the belly; for it is what goes into a man that ruins him. By avoiding murderous food, we may hope to become centenarians. And why not? The golden streets will not be torn up and we need be in no indecent haste to travel even on them. The satisfactions of this life are just beginning for us; and we shall be wise to endure this world for as long as possible.

And sleep is good – long sleep and often; and your age and mine permit us to indulge in it without the sneers of the lark or the cock or the dawn.

I pray you, sir, therefore, accept my homage as the philosopher that you are and my assurance of that high esteem indicated by my faithful imitation of your virtues. I am

    With the most distinguished consideration,

    With the sincerest esteem,

    With the most affectionate good wishes,

Sir,

Your proud

Humble,

Obedient

GRANDADDY

LADY (ANN) BUTLER (1876–1953)

mother of 'Rab' Butler

Ann Smith, daughter of a Scottish Presbyterian family, was unconventional and extrovert and enjoyed a happy marriage lasting more than fifty years to Montagu Butler, who came of a long line of distinguished academics and public servants. The eldest of their four children, Richard Austen, known as 'Rab' (a future Cabinet minister and architect of the 1944 Education Act), was born at Attock, a fort guarding the confluence of the rivers Indus and Kabul, in 1902.

Ann brought 'Rab' home to England when he was eight but, untypically of her class, did not abandon him for years on end, although she returned to India without him in 1916, the year he went to Marlborough. She recalled her heartache in a letter to him, dated Boxing Day, 1917.

... when I left you at the gate across the fields ... The whole place looked so lovely and I often wonder how ever I'd the courage to leave you.

But Ann was not a woman to bemoan her lot, as this splendid account of the Armistice of November 1918 shows.

Campbellpore
November 13th 1918

Dearest of Rabs, I wanted to write to you yesterday – the 12th. – the Day of Peace and Victory. It's too thrilling, & bewildering also. I sat down to write on the sunny verandah after the excitement of the earlier morning. For Dads got the Reuter at 9, when were at breakfast & instantly sent it to the Judge & Policeman while he went himself to the Mess. On his return, he & the Judge, the Policeman & Captain Mumtaz & me (to represent women's war work!) all got into Mumtaz' car, & drove to the School. There Dads announced Victory to cheering children & youths, who all followed us in our procession round the Civil Station & City. It was like an election campaign; – the car proceeding slowly & surrounded by shouting crowds robust. They carried an effigy of the Kaiser on a bed, for I forgot to mention that by 9.30 the Cadets here – British rankers training for officers – came up to cheer us and everybody in front of the house. And they brought the Kaiser on a stretcher, covered with the mysterious letters, which in ambulance work mean 'desperate case'. The Cadets beat their wash hand basins & baths with sticks, & sang patriotic songs. So the schoolboys imitated this on their effigy, at which many people looked doubtedfully, the rows of the funerals caused by the flu being still fresh in their memories.

There was then a meeting at the Mess, when Dads organised everybody to get sports and excitements ready by 3.30. Rather an effort & very successful indeed. The Cadets had races, ditto the schoolboys & the camel corps, while there was a hockey tournament on the adjoining ground.

Police v. 2/19th Punjabis won by 2/19th
40th Pathans v. 2/46th Punjabis won by 2/46th
Finals at 5 won by 2/19th

Then the O.C. Station Col Platt made a short speech & thanked Dads & the War League, whose funds stood the tea & prizes. The Cadet Unit Mess provided the tea, arranged by nice Sgt Scuddar, their Mess Sgt. I then presented the prizes – jolly good ones. The hockey team got Rs 100, the camel tug of war 40rs & the races were 15 & 10 for 1st prizes.

We motored back & after dinner went to the Cadet Unit sing song, which was quite amusing. Now our scheme is to give a dinner on Friday for Peace & Victory. We shall be 24 altogether & I will arrange it in 3 tables. The servants are highly pleased. They've always been keen on the war, & the Indian hates being hustled & denied as we have had to press him. Now this dinner redounds to our & their glory, so they are full of preparations. Dads thinks we must give fizz, but whatever happens it will be a succès, & speeches will be made. It might be rather fun.

I do feel just now most of all for people like Aunt Winnie & others who have just at the end, lost their men. And indeed anyone who's lost people like Uncle George has, for now all the world is coming home rejoicing, & this makes the blank worse for them.

Dads was awfully amused about Mr. Jelf talking to you at Cambridge, as he says he never liked him at the Grays[?].

It's awfully nice you have this fishing rod & all, I've written to Nan & sent her raisins. They were topping over the holiday. I have sent such a lot of sweets, crys fruit, raisins & cheese home to all of you. I do hope they arrive. Most fortunate that the Coonoor sweets did just at the right moment.

Every day the craze is for the Baby to make a motor with all the deck & garden chairs. He is seated in it now, burbulling all the route he means to go & all that happens. Nannie made tricolour flags, as we had not time to make a Union Jack; Besides we had yours from the Wick – do you remember.

All my love, dearest,

<u>M.</u>

VIRGINIA WOOLF (1882–1941)

novelist, essayist, critic

One of the most innovative novelists of the early twentieth century, Virginia Woolf and her husband, Leonard, were a cornerstone of the Bloomsbury group of writers, painters and thinkers. She suffered long periods of severe depression, and drowned herself in the Sussex Ouse. Although she was childless, she liked children. She wanted them to be observant. Nigel Nicolson tells how, at a party, she might suddenly shoo away the grown-ups and turn to questioning a group of young people gathering near by.

"Tell me, what's your French teacher like?"
Nervously, "Oh, she's quite nice."
"No, no. I don't mean that. What sort of *shoes* does she wear?"

This is a letter she wrote to Elaine Robson, aged six, daughter of Juliette Alvin, the cellist and music therapist, and W. A. Robson of the London School of Economics. The original letter is written in capital letters.

My dear Elaine,

I like your poem and your story very much indeed. I have not seen a rabbit washing his ceiling but yesterday I saw a hare who was making a warm bed for his winter lodging in the marsh. He had just laid down a nice blanket made of thistledown when he saw me and ran away. His bed was quite hot and I put a mushroom there for him to eat. The marsh is full of mushrooms. I wish you and Daddy and Mummy were all here to pick them and then we could cook them and have them for supper. I also saw a kingfisher. His bed is in the bank of the river but I have never found it. Sally has had a thorn in her paw and we have had to poultice it. At last the thorn came out and her paw is only as big as a penny bun. It was as big as a soup-plate. Mitzi had a macaroon for breakfast this morning. When you are in London will you come to tea with us and make a binding for your lovely poem. Do you like writing prose or poetry best. This typewriter cannot spell and sometimes uses wrong type. XXXXXX Uncle Leonard sends his love. Sally has just barked her love also and Mitzi bit me in the ear, which means she sends her love too.

Your affectionate aunt Virginia

SIR PELHAM GRENVILLE WODEHOUSE
(1881–1975)
humorous writer

P.G. Wodehouse, son of a Hong Kong judge, was educated at Dulwich College and worked briefly in banking before becoming a writer. His first novel was published in 1902; he was working on his last when he died. He lived much in America and France. World War II found him and his wife stranded at Le Touquet (he was incurably optimistic but no judge of politics) and they spent the war in Germany. There he foolishly made broadcasts, which were misunderstood, to America, although continuing his genial sagas of Jeeves, Lord Emsworth, Psmith and others. During this time there were no letters so the Wodehouses did not hear of the untimely death of Leonora Cazalet, his step-daughter, until 1945. She was a most charming, much-loved person. Here he writes in 1920. She is sixteen, and war and separation and early deaths have just ceased, and light hearts are in season.

Quinton Farm
Felixstowe
Suffolk
7th August 1920

My darling angel Snorkles,

At last I'm able to write to you! I finished the novel yesterday, and I wish you were here to read it, as I think it's the best comic one I've done. It's not meant to be in the same class as *The Little Warrior*, but as a farce I think it's pretty well all the mustard. I've done it in such a hurry, though, that there may be things wrong with it. Still, I'm going to keep it by me for at least two weeks before sending it off to America, so perhaps you'll be able to see it after all before it goes. If not, you can read the original MS.

I don't suppose it will sell as a serial in England. They want such stodgy stuff over here, most of the magazines, and the *Strand* and the *Grand* are both full up with my stuff for months to come.

I have now got three more Archie stories to do and then I shall have worked off all my present contracts. I haven't got a plot yet for the tenth Archie story, but they are using a golf story of mine in the Christmas *Strand*, which will give me a fair amount of time to think of one.

Mummie went off to London yesterday, and I am all alone here and rather blue. I leave on Friday and I hope we shall soon get a flat in town.

Mummie has taken up golf and is very keen on it and is really getting quite good. You must start as soon as you can . . .

Don't you think this is a good line in the book. Chap who's always thinking himself ill says to chap who's having a row with him 'My face hurts!' Other chap says 'You can't expect a face like that not to hurt!' I thought it was not only droll, but whimsical and bizarre, but Mummie said it was obvious! No human power however, will induce me to cut it out.

I've got another good line. Chap is asked if he identifies the hero, with whom he has had a row. Hero has been found in the house late at night and they think he is a burglar. He says 'I am Sam Marlowe.' They turn to the other fellow and say 'Do you identify him?' and the other fellow says 'I suppose so, I can't imagine a man saying he was Samuel Marlowe unless he knew it could be proved against him.' Somewhat humorous and not altogether free from espièglerie, I think, or am I wrong?

A man has just written to me asking if I will dramatize his new novel, which he says he wrote in imitation of my stuff. I had read a preview of his novel, and had thought it was just the sort of thing to read and pinch situations from. And so we go on, each helping the other.

As a matter of fact, I really am becoming rather a blood these days. In a review of *Weddings Bells* at the Playhouse the critic says 'So-and-so is good as a sort of P.G. Wodehouse character.' And in a review of a book in the *Times*, they say, 'The author at times reverts to the P.G. Wodehouse manner.' This, I need scarcely point out to you, is jolly Fame. Once they begin to refer to you in that casual way as if everybody must know who you are all is well. It does my old heart good.

My golf is terrific now. I seldom miss. Tom Irwin, one of your trustees for the money which I hope to find some way of pinching in the near future, was down here and has given me a new putter, which produces wonderful results.

I'm glad you liked *The Little White Bird*. One of my favourite books.

Georgia O'Ramey is singing 'Galahad' in Cochran's new revue. Isn't it darned cheek! I want heavy damages and all that sort of thing. What scares me is that she has probably pinched 'Cleopatra', 'Very Good Girl on Sunday', and 'Blood' from *Springtime* as well. It begins to look like a pretty thin sort of world if tons of hams unfit for human consumption are going to lift one's best things out of shows and use them themselves without even a kind smile.

Well, pip pip and good-bye-ee and so forth,

Your loving
Plummie

SIR HAROLD NICOLSON (1886–1968)

diplomat, politician, literary critic, diarist and biographer

Sir Harold Nicolson wrote many books – *King George V*, *Some People*, *Good Behaviour*, and other works. He was married to Victoria Sackville-West. Their country home was at Sissinghurst, Kent, where they created a remarkable garden. They had two sons, Benedict and Nigel. The latter edited his parents' letters, and wrote of them in *Portrait of a Marriage* – a frank account of a very unusual one. Nigel Nicolson was nine years old when his father wrote him this letter:

GULAHEK, PERSIA
16 July 1926

I do hope that you won't make Mummy nervous by being too wild. Of course men must work and women must weep, but all the same, I hope you will remember that Mummy is a frightful coward and does fuss dreadfully about you. It is a good rule always to ask before you do anything awfully dangerous. Thus, if you say, 'Mummy, may I try and walk on the roof of the greenhouse on my stilts?' she will probably say, 'Of course, darling,' since she is not in any way a narrow minded woman. And if you say, 'Mummy, may I light a little fire in my bed?' she will again say, 'Certainly, Nigel.' It is only that she likes being asked about these things beforehand.

DR CHARLES MACPHERSON (1870–1927)

organist

Benjamin Britten, who was to become a distinguished composer and founder of the Aldeburgh Festival, wrote at the age of twelve to Dr Macpherson, submitting an early work. Britten, who was a good pupil at school, especially at maths, music and games, must have found Dr Macpherson's advice all the more gratifying for needing no effort to follow. And he was not put off by Macpherson's phlegmatic reaction to his youthful composition.

8 Amen Court, EC4
14 Dec: 1926

Dear Master Britten,

Here is your M.S. I hope you will go on writing whenever you have the chance. Hear all the music you can, and when you begin serious study you will find out a lot of things for yourself. Solving your own difficulties in music, without slavish imitation of others, or a too great insistence on some personal fancy or mannerism is one of the best things to have for composing.

<u>But</u>, meanwhile, learn all your lessons, not forgetting to play games!

I'm sure you will do well if you take things seriously. There is nothing done without hard work; but I fancy you have this gift.

Yrs very sincerely
<u>Charles Macpherson</u>

DAVID HERBERT LAWRENCE (1885–1930)

writer

D.H. Lawrence, son of a Nottinghamshire coal-miner and a teacher, became a professional writer in 1911. He wrote novels and short stories prolifically, also poems, plays and travel books. In addition to this prodigious output he wrote hundreds of letters and maintained affectionate contact with his extended family.

This anecdote comes from a tape recording by Lawrence's niece Peggy (later Mrs Margaret Needham), who created a museum in his honour at Nottingham. One day, on returning home from school, she heard him in the parlour and burst in joyfully to hear about his travels. But her mother said homework came first and she was sent to the kitchen where, eventually, Uncle Bert joined her, asking if he could help. Peggy explained that the next day she had to lead a debate on the motion: Experience teaches more than Learning. Lawrence took pencil and paper and wrote fluently without pause for ten minutes. His argument was that learning was suited to facts and things in books whereas one needed experience to deal with the important things: human relationships and marriage, for example. Next day, Peggy's side won the debate 'with a little help from Lawrence'.

Here is a letter to Harwood Brewster, the young daughter of friends.

Villa Mirenda
Scandicci
Firenze
15 May 1927

My dear Harwood

Here are a few ribbons – your Aunt Frieda got them yesterday in Florence – not the same as the bunch I bought myself for you – but who knows what villains or villainesses are bedizened up with them now, those others. If these aren't quite what you want for your hair, you can tie up charming bouquets with them to present to your mother's elderly-lady-guests. Otherwise there is always dear, dumb, smiling Rose to embellish, who never says a word, thank God!

I am wondering what is happening to you. You've been a full month in that hotel: at least your parents have. Heavens, what waifs and strays! I suppose you'll land in another 'beautiful pretentious villa.' It's become a habit.

Have you begun bathing? It's rather cold here, after the thunder storms, that is compared to the heat before. But I feel better when it's *fresco*. The garden is full of roses, and the *poderi* full of peas and beans and *carciofi* [artichokes], which is all to the good: really a happy vegetarian moment.

Well, I hope things are happening nicely for you all. Be an angel, and hold your chin up.

lo zio [uncle]
David

HARRY S. TRUMAN (1884–1972)

thirty-third President of the United States

Harry S. Truman sprang to international fame when he succeeded to the presidency of the United States of America on the sudden death of Franklin D. Roosevelt in April 1945. A few months later it was he, with the consent of Clement Attlee, Britain's prime minister following the defeat of Churchill and the Conservatives, who took the decision to drop the atomic bombs on Japan which ended World War II.

Truman married his childhood sweetheart – they met at Sunday school in 1890 – in 1919, following his service on the Western Front in World War I. They had one daughter, Mary Margaret, born 1924. It was his practice to write daily to his wife – 1,200 letters are preserved in his archive and they are the ones that survived! By the time she was only four years old, his daughter was being urged to keep up the habit of writing daily to her father, for he was often away from home at summer camps with his old regiment.

Ft. Riley
Saturday 16 July 27

Dear Little Daughter,

I received your letter this noon along with your mothers and it was very fine. I was glad to get it because another gentleman at my table had just received one just like it from his little girl. There are two little yellow haired girls in this same barrack. One of them is four and the other is two and they have a fine time, playing together. The four year old one ran across the porch yesterday and fell down. She bumped her nose just like you do when you fall and she cried just like you do. Her father is a nice looking cavalry captain. He picked her up and swore at the government for having him live where the boards in his front porch are loose, so his little girl would fall. I told him that my little girl always picked a gravel road to fall on. These little girls have dolls and tea tables and scooters. You'd have a fine time with them.

Kiss your mother and write me again.

Your daddy.

Camp Rigby, Minn.
July 20, 1932

Dear Daughter:

Your fine letter came this morning and your dad was surely glad to get it. I do wish you and your mother were here, in spite of the cannon. A little boy about your age came out to the firing point yesterday and when the guns went off he almost climbed the flag pole. I think he was more scared than you'd have been. Someday I hope you wont mind them and will come and watch your daddy shoot and see how it is done.

I am glad you are practising because I would be disappointed if someone should say that the reason Margaret Truman can't play is because her daddy is trying to teach her and he doesn't know how. I want you to know how but I can't do it for you. You have to work for yourself if you expect to accomplish anything, and I surely want you to be as good as the best in everything you undertake except smoking cigarettes, and I hope you'll never do that. I've never yet seen a smoking woman that I'd have around me for a minute.

I am glad you are walking everywhere and I hope you'll be entirely well when I get home next Sunday.

Kiss your mamma for me and tell her I still look for letters.

Your loving
Dad

Here are two more pictures of your dad.

CONRAD AIKEN (1889–1973)

American poet, novelist and critic

Grandson of the Elizabeth who wrote the birthday letter, Conrad Aiken was educated at Harvard where he roomed with T.S. Eliot and started a lifelong friendship. He spent much time in England between the wars and, from London, wrote for the *New Yorker* as 'Samuel Jeake jnr'. (He lived at Jeake's House, Rye, in East Sussex.) Already a Fellow in American Letters of the Library of Congress, in 1950 Aiken became Poet in Residence, a job he described to his daughter Joan as 'not exactly fictitious, but . . . slightly imaginary'.

Of his three children by his first marriage, John turned to science, and Jane Aiken Hodge and Joan (b. 1924) became successful writers.

In this letter Conrad Aiken thanks his younger daughter, aged nine, for the birthday poem she has sent him. First, the poem.

The moon is shining faintly gold
Up in the evening sky
I wonder how it keeps its hold
And how it sails so slowly by

The clouds are flocking, flocking
Around the rosy pink
The wind is rocking, rocking
The sun away, I think

The trees are slowly stirring
You hear the fountain splash
The evening wind is purring
The birds no longer dash.

The owls are not yet calling
The sun has just been blown
O'er dew that's softly falling
On grass that's to be mown.

Jeake's House
Rye
18 August 33

Dear Joan,

Thank you very much for the lovely letter, which came on my birthday, and for the poem, which so delighted me that I'm learning it by heart, and for the two beautiful drawings. It was the nicest birthday present I had. And the poem is REALLY lovely – I particularly like the last stanza – and of the last stanza I particularly like the last line – and any poet or poetess who can end a poem with the best stanza and end the best stanza with the best line is a good poet! So many poets begin well – and keep it up *fairly* well for a stanza or two – but then get tireder and tireder and feebler and feebler and finally just stop out of sheer exhaustion: by which time their readers have usually been exhausted too. But your poem gets better as it goes along – and that's the way it should be. Have you got any others that you could send me? I'd love to have some more . . . What fun it is to have so many poets in the family, isn't it? Pretty soon we'll be able to make an Aiken anthology. And we all seem to begin so young. I began at nine – Jane wrote her celebrated epic when she was six, if I remember right – John too, I believe, achieved a few verses when he was very young – but he and Jane both seem to have neglected the art lately. Perhaps if you spoke very sternly to them they'd do their duty again . . . How nice that you can swim now, with a hand under your chin – and how nice that you *like* bathing – as for me, I find the sea very cold and large and so often it has large waves and so often too it is full of sharp stones and almost always it seems too far away to get to: and so I almost never go. I think it's nicer to look at from the study window . . . The cat, whose name is Squidge, or Squodge, or Squadge, or Zubo, or Squorryongs, or Woggatzibs, or Warryonganimbs, or Warryibbotzobbotz, has just come into the dining room and is lying on a rug in a pool of sunlight and washing his right front paw with extreme care, almost, but not quite, shutting his eyes. I wish you could meet him, he's a VERY nice cat . . . Perhaps some time you will come to Jeake's House and be introduced to him . . . Now I must stop, for I'm writing this on the dining room table, and the lunch is arriving and wants the table all to herself.

Lots of love
Cahoun

Conrad Aiken writes a birthday letter to this same daughter, Joan. Unfortunately, her birthday is on 4 September – but many fathers do not do as well as this.

> *Cunard White Star*
> '*Scythia*'
> Sept 6 37

. . . Well my beloved Fiddles, as you see I'm once more writing on ship notepaper, but Ho Ho that's the joke, for I'm by no means on a ship, and not even AT a Ship (though it still rocks at the pier of Leith) but, believe it or not, in the study of Jeake's House, with the dart-board just above my head and the mast of the Saxon visible beyond the rooftops, And the occasion for this letter, you will be astonished to hear is the rumour that you are about to have a birthday. And as I'm one of these people who get fidgety waiting for events to come, and rush in too early always, like going for trains two days ahead of time, why, I write to you <u>now</u>, and get it all over and done with. See? Of course. Anyway, it's the early worm that gets the bird, as the poet said in a dark moment, which all goes to prove something pretty tremendous if only we could find out what it was . . . Rye plods on in its groove, and we went to Hastings to see a very comic baseball match last week, and we've had a torrent of visitors and folk to meals, bad cess to 'em, but now they've gone, and the Mackecks have sailed away to Italy, and this afternoon Ed is coming with his car to drive us over to Canterbury where, I believe the idea is <u>not</u> to look at cathedrals – nothing so mundane – but naturally to eat oysters. Yum yum. If you never hear from me again, lo[o]k me up in a small oyster bar up a cobbled alley two blocks east of the cathedral gateway, I'll still be there, up to my chin in empty oyster shells.

Well, that's all for today, and I hope you're having a galumpshus time up
there in your rivers and things, and Mary joins me in premature
congratulations, and the enclosed is just for fun. Lots of loves
                          from Cahoun

Mary was his second wife.

F. SCOTT FITZGERALD (1896–1940)

novelist, short-story writer

Fitzgerald's success with his first novel, *This Side of Paradise*, at twenty-four, enabled him to marry Zelda Sayre, the sparkling daughter of a wealthy upper-class family. The couple became fashionable, representing youth, glamour, America, the Jazz Age. Life was a non-stop party; drink became a problem to them both. Zelda moved towards mental breakdown but Scott went on working. His output was vast and he was the bread-winner not only for Zelda and himself but for their much-loved daughter, Frances Scott Fitzgerald, known as Scottie. He was determined she should have the finest possible education and wrote to her frequently, exhorting her to make the best of herself, and not to make the same mistakes that he – and her mother – had made.

Grove Park Inn
Asheville, North Carolina
[Summer 1935]

Scottina:

It was fine seeing you, and I liked you a lot (this is aside from loving you which I always do). You are nicer to adults – you are emerging from that rather difficult time in girls, 12–15 usually, but you are emerging I think rather early – probably at 14 or so. You have one good crack coming but – well.

'Daddy the prophet!' I can hear you say in scorn. I wish to God I wasn't so right usually about you. When I wrote that 'news-sheet' with events left out, you know – the letter that puzzled you – and headed it 'Scottie Loses Head', it was because I saw it coming. I knew that your popularity with two or three dazed adolescent boys would convince you that you were at least

the Queen of Sheba, and that you would 'lose your head'. What shape this
haywire excursion would take I didn't know – I couldn't have guessed it
would be writing a series of indiscreet letters to a gossipy and indiscreet boy
who would show them to the person for whom they were *not* meant
(Understand: I don't blame Andrew[1] too much – the fault was yours – he
didn't, will you notice, put into writing an analysis of his best friends of his
own sex!)

However, that's of no seriousness. But I think that the next kick will be a
bad one – but you will survive, and after that you will manage your affairs
better. To avoid such blows you almost *have* to have them yourself so you
can begin to think of others as valuing themselves, possibly, quite as much
as you do yourself. So I'm not afraid of it for you. I don't want it to be so
bad that it will break your self-confidence, which is attractive and is fine (if)
founded on positive virtues, work, courage, etc., but if you are selfish it had
better be broken early. If you are unselfish you can keep it always – and it is
a nice thing to have. I didn't know till 15 that there was anyone in the world
except me, and it cost me *plenty*.

Signs and portents of your persistent conceit: Mrs. Owens[2] said to me
(and Mrs. Owens loves you) 'For the first time in a long while Scottie was
nice, and not a burden as I expected. It was really nice to be with her.'

Because, I guess, for the first time you entered into *their* lives, humble lives
of struggling people, instead of insisting that they enter into yours – a
chance they never had, of belonging to 'high society'. Before, you had let
them be aware of what *you* were doing (not in any snobbish sense, because
heaven knows I'd have checked you on that) – but because you never
considered or pretended to consider their lives, their world at all – your own
activities seemed of so much more overwhelming importance to you! *You
did not use one bit of your mind, one little spot!* to think what *they* were thinking, or
help *them!*

You went to Norfolk and gave out the information (*via* the Taylors, *via*
Annabel, *via* mother) that you were going to Dobbs. That doesn't matter
save as indicative of a show-off frame of mind. You know it was highly
tentative. It was a case, again, of boasting, of 'promoting yourself.' But
those signs of one big catastrophe (it'll come – I want to minimize it for
you, but it can't be prevented because only experience can teach) are less

---

[1] Andrew Turnbull.
[2] Fitzgerald's secretary.

important than your failure to realize that you are a *young member of the human race*, who has not proved itself in any way but the most superficial manner. (I have seen 'popular girls' of 15 become utterly *déclassé* in six months because they were essentially selfish.) You and Peaches[1] (who isn't selfish, I think) had a superficial head-start with prettiness, but you will find more and more that less pretty girls will be attaching the solider, more substantial boys as the next two years will show. Both you and Peaches are intelligent but both of you will be warped by his early attention, *and something tells me she won't lose her head*, she hasn't the 'gift of gab' as you have – her laughter and her silence takes the place of much. That's why I wish to God you would write something when you have time – if only a one act play about how girls act in the bath house, in a tent, on a train going to camp.

I grow weary, but I probably won't write again for a month. Don't answer this, justifying yourself – *of course* I know you're doing the best you 'can'.

The points of the letter are:

1st   You did spill over, rashly!

2nd   You are getting over the selfish period – thank God!

3rd   But it'll take one more big kick, and I want it to be mild, so your backside won't suffer too much.

4th   I wish you'd get your mind off your precious self enough to write me a one act play about other people – what they say and how they behave.

With *dearest* love,

Your simply so-perfect too-too

Daddy

Please, turn back and read this letter over! It is too packed with considered thoughts to digest the first time. Like Milton – oh yeah!

---

[1] A close friend of Scottie's.

J.R.R. TOLKEIN (1892–1973)

philologist, academic, critic, novelist

Tolkien was born in South Africa but educated in England, graduating from Merton College, Oxford, where he became Professor of Anglo-Saxon, 1925–1945. He was a close friend of C.S. Lewis – see page 211. Tolkien is internationally famous for the books in which he created a country of his own, having its own language. *The Lord of the Rings* has become something of a cult, and graffiti, observed on Oxford's golden walls, proclaimed 'Tolkien is Hobbit-Forming'. This letter to his second son, Michael, gives advice, less fancifully, concerning rugby football. Chris is Michael's younger brother, and both are at the Oratory School in Berkshire.

29 Northmoor Road, Oxford
3 October 1937

Dearest Mick,

It was nice to have a letter from you. I hope all is going well. I thought the new flats looked as if they would be presentable when furnished. It is good of you to keep a kindly eye on Chris, as far as you can. I expect he will make a mess of things to begin with, but he ought soon to find his bearings and be no more trouble to you or himself.

I am sorry and surprised that you are not (yet) in the team. But many a man ends up in it and even with colours, who is rejected at first. It was so with me – and for same reason; too light. But one day I decided to make up for weight by (legitimate) ferocity, and I ended up a house captain at end of that season, I got my colours the next. But I got rather damaged – among other things having my tongue nearly cut out – and as I am on the whole rather luckier than you, I should really be quite happy if you remain uninjured though not in the team! But God bless you and keep you anyway. There is no very special news. Mummy seems to have taken to car-riding. We have been two since you left, and I have now got to take her, P. and J.B. out this afternoon instead of writing. So this must be all for the moment. With much love indeed.

Your own
Father.

E.B. WHITE (1899–1985)
author and journalist

E.B.White's name is indelibly associated with the *New Yorker* magazine, whose first fiction editor, Katharine Angell, he married in 1929. Their son, Joel, to whom the following letter was written, was born one year later. E.B. White won many literary awards, and published nearly twenty books of essays, poems and stories. These included the notably successful children's tale *Charlotte's Web*, and a collection with James Thurber, *Is Sex Necessary?*

The Grosvenor
35 Fifth Avenue
New York
[June 23, 1940]

Dear Joel,

From my hotel window I can see the apartment building on Eighth Street where we used to live when you were a baby. I can also see the trees of Washington Square, and the backyards of the houses on Ninth Street with their little gardens of potted plants and trellises. The Sixth Avenue Elevated is gone, and New York looks very different on that account. People still like to come out in their sun-suits on Sunday morning and sun themselves in their roof gardens and they still spend a good deal of time taking dogs out for a walk, not realising how lucky they are that there are no porcupines. Everybody that I talk to is very gloomy about the war and about the defeat of France, but that is true everywhere today. In Radio City, where we used to skate, there is an open-air restaurant, with people sitting at little tables under big green umbrellas. The fountain is going and makes a great noise.

How has everything been going in Maine? I miss you a lot and wish I could be there right now, although my hay fever bothers me less in the city than in the country. Is Barney[1] coming to cut the hay? I hope so. And did you get any Barred Rock chicks from Mr. Sylvester[2]? Tell me all about these things, and whether you have caught any fish.

There is a church right opposite the hotel, and every afternoon the chimes ring at about five o'clock when people are coming home from work. It reminds me of being a student at Cornell, where the chimes in the library tower used to ring every afternoon toward the end of day. I suppose right now the bell in the church in Brooklin is ringing, too, five hundred miles from here.

Tell Mother that everything is going along all right, and that I'll try to get a good deal of work done in the next few days so that I'll be able to be back in Maine soon. I'm still hoping that you and I can take a little camping trip this summer, so you better keep your ax sharpened up and your boots oiled. I hope you'll help Mother as much as you can while I'm away, and write me if you get time.

Affectionately,
Dad

---

[1] Barney Steele, who had a team of horses. Joel sometimes took the reins.
[2] A storekeeper.

LETTERS FROM THE SECOND WORLD WAR
1939–1945

Letters in this anthology from World War I were written by men on active service. The first here tells of experiences at home.

Olive Lumley has been evacuated from Bermondsey, east London, to Llanelli, South Wales. She is sixteen when she receives the news that her parents have been bombed out. Both have survived. For a short while no details reach her. She asks everyone she can for further news, and in response her father sends her an admirably clear and methodical account of what happened, moving in its self-control, which he allows to falter momentarily in a tribute to his compatriots.

The first page of **Mr Lumley**'s letter concerns photographic techniques, to steady his nerve, perhaps. This page is omitted.

65 Napier Road
Enfield
Middx
30–4–41

Dear Olive,

. . .

Mummy and myself feel a bit better now after the shock of losing our home. I don't think Mummy told you the full story. Well I was on duty in Bermondsey that night, and London had a terrific 'Blitz' the worst we've ever had and we've had some. I and my male staff were kept busy putting out incendiaries most of the night and there were great fires all around us. Of course, a number of H.E.'s were dropped but on the whole B'sey didn't do so bad. Mummy & most of the neighbours were out on the look-out for incendiaries in Devonshire Rd and Mummy went indoors about midnight to make cups of tea. In fact she had just made it when she was blown on to her knees in the kitchen and landed on the floor between the gas cooker and the 'acme' wringer, the whole house at the same time tumbling about her head. It seems that the gas cooker & wringer took the weight & saved Mummy being completely crushed, but she was held by the neck & the knees. She couldn't move her head but her arms were free. She thought it was all 'up' and then after a few minutes decided that the thing to do was to call for help. This she did and at the same time she heard the Mansells' calling to her (Mrs. Mansell was not at home but away at Woking). Eventually a reserve party arrived and after about an hour and a half they got her out bruised, a few slight cuts and suffering a bit from shock. She was wrapped up in blankets and taken in an ambulance to a first-aid post adjoining the South Eastern Hospital for children in Sydenham Rd. She got a sister at the F.A.P. to 'phone through to get hold of me and I got a message that our house had been bombed but that Mrs. Lumley was safe about 8.0 AM. It also said – this message – that Mummy was at Kelvin Grove School Rest Centre. I thought that our house had just been blasted and that Mummy and the neighbours had had to clear out for the time being. When I got to Devonshire Rd & saw the destruction I got a shock, because I didn't think it was possible to have got anybody out alive. Mr. & Mrs. Simmonds were got out about 7.00 AM. They were injured and taken to S.E. Hosp Sydenham afterwards being removed to Sutton Emergency Hosp. They are going on fairly well. Mrs Simmonds had her spine badly bruised & Mr Simmonds was hurt about the eyes. Mr. & Mrs. Town were killed, Mr. & Andy Stockwell were killed. Miss Davies & Mr. & Mrs. Constable Senr were all killed. Mr. Hodges was badly injured, Mrs. Hodges very seriously injured. We don't know about Tony. Phyllis Davies badly injured. Mr. & Mrs. Constable junr both badly injured. You see the 'mine' fell in Town's garden just at the back of their house, so that 164, 166 & 168 were completely wrecked, so were 170, 172, 174. Bastin's Weller's & Mansell's houses were very badly blasted but did not collapse so no one was hurt on that side of us. Almost everything that stood upright in the gardens was laid flat, it looked a terrible sight & the ground was strewn with bits of the parachute & its cord from the 'mine'. They are colossal things. They are 8' 6" long by 2' 9" diameter & weigh something over 2 tons. They make practically no noise in falling but being so big and falling slower than an ordinary bomb they can be seen. It is said that Mr. Hodges and Andy were in the garden & that Mr. Hodges saw it coming. He shouted 'Look out' & rushed indoors flinging himself full length in the passage between back door and hall.

The following days I organised a gang from B'sey with vans & we managed to get something out. We've rescued some clothes, books, bedding & tinned food, we got the sitting room bookcase & 3 piece suite out in reasonable condition but the piano is smashed up & all the dining room stuff, likewise the bedrooms. We found Mummy's hand-bags with money & also our valuable documents, so we haven't done so bad considering the nature of the smash. Of course I've put in a substantial claim under the Govt compensation Scheme, but what we ever get remains to be seen. We don't want to stay at Ponders End its not comfortable enough and its a long dreary journey up to B'sey. Mrs. Mansell has taken a flat in London Road Forest Hill & as its bigger than she wants she has made suggestions to us which Mummy regards rather favourably. Anyway you'll hear later what we do. We don't want to start a home again till after the war, at least not a home as we've known it. Both Mummy & I were very keen about our place at Devonshire Rd. and we felt it badly although of course we were very thankful that it was no worse. I might have been there & you might have been there & I think if we had we might have been in the dining room & nobody could possibly [have] survived in there. The gas-cooker & wringer that saved Mummy were both badly smashed although they didn't collapse to the floor so you see it was a matter of inches . . .

Don't <u>you</u> worry about anything. We're not penniless and try not to get restless at having to wait until next year to go to college. Don't forget we're all looking forward to 'after the war' and then you'll be ever so glad you stuck it out. I should be ever so proud of you if you do well in your career, so come on chins up.

Much love from Mummy & myself.

Daddy

Pat Baker was four when her father, **Frederick Lorraine Formidable Baker**, known as Ted, was killed in action on the Greek island of Leros in November 1943. A year previously he had written three letters, one to each of his children. Pat's mother gave her the letter below when she was fourteen. In Tamasin Day-Lewis's anthology, *Last Letters Home*, Pat says, 'It made me think about my life and how to live it . . . It's as if he's still alive . . . I can't remember anything else he ever said to me. That letter filled that void . . . I know I'm far luckier than a lot of daughters whose fathers never said things like that.'

Sunday, 4th October 1942

My Darling little Pat,

I have been thinking things over while waiting for my boat, and as I might not return, I think it is only right that you should have a letter from me which you can keep, to remember me by. I am writing this assuming you are now grown up, as you will not receive this till then. I can picture you as a lovely girl, very happy with lots of boy friends. I am finding it very hard to write this as I may never see you at this stage. You have always been the pride and joy of my life. I have loved you more than my life and at all times. As mother has told you perhaps, I was always afraid of losing you. Now the tables have turned the other way and I might be the one to get lost. But do not let this upset you if this is the case, as the love for a father only lasts up to the time a girl finds the man she wants and gets married. Well, darling, when this time arises I hope you find the right one and he will not only be a good husband to you, but will also make up for the fatherly love you have missed. At all times, lovie, be a pal to mother and look after her, do what you can to make her happy, as she has been and will always be, I am sure, the best little mother you will find on this earth. Don't be selfish or catty, remember there are others in the world as well as you. Try not to talk about people as this gets you disliked. When the pulling to pieces starts, walk out or turn a deaf ear, it will pay in the long run. Above all I want you to be a sport, to take up swimming, dancing and all the games in life you can get so much fun out of. Mother, I am sure, will do her best for you and see you get all the instruction she can afford. Always try to be a sister to Peter and John [Pat's cousin], they may pull your leg about different things. But the best way after all is to ignore them and do what you can for them. You will win in the end and be the best of pals. Well, darling, there is no more I can say, but to look after yourself where men are concerned, be wise and quick witted and only believe half they say, of course till you get the right one. Remember me as your dad and pal who worshipped the ground you walked on. Please don't do anything that will upset mother, and I shouldn't like you to. I will close now, my little ray of sunshine.

Always loving you.

Your Loving,

Father.

xxxxxxxxxxxx

DWIGHT DAVID EISENHOWER (1890–1969)

army general, thirty-fourth President of the USA

General Eisenhower had a distinguished record in World War II, culminating in his being chosen to lead the Allied armies on D-Day, 6 June 1944, the cross-Channel invasion of Europe which brought victory the following year. After two years as commander of NATO land forces he stood in 1952 for the US presidency, as a Republican, won, and was re-elected in 1956. He also had a flair for writing to very small girls. This is to his niece, Ruthie.

DDE/wm
6 April, 1943

Dear Ruthie,

I enjoyed your letter. I know exactly what you said. I am astonished that you have made such progress since I last saw you. Since I cannot write as well as you do, I will have to have this done on the typewriter, so your Mother may have to read it to you.

I know that by the time I come home that beautiful blue velvet dress that you got a year ago for Christmas, will be far too small: but please keep it because I think that is the best looking dress I ever saw in my life and I want to see it again.

With lots of love.

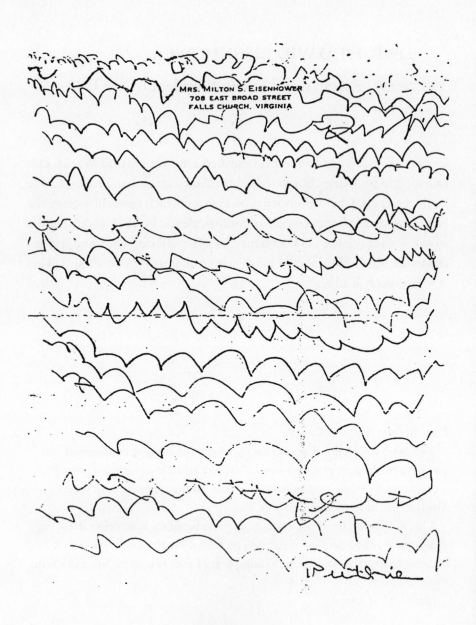

MRS. MILTON S. EISENHOWER
708 EAST BROAD STREET
FALLS CHURCH, VIRGINIA

Ruthie's letter

FRANÇOIS TRUFFAUT (1932–1984)

film director

Truffaut, an only child, was moved from school to school, constantly truanting. His friend Robert Lachenay (two years his senior) and he developed an ingenious method of spending the whole morning reading in Robert's bedroom, and the afternoon at the cinema. Robert would silently let François in, then shout loudly, 'Bye, Mum,' clatter noisily down the stairs, only to re-enter the flat by another door and creep back to his bedroom. The two boys pawned a typewriter stolen from Robert's father's office to afford books and cinema. The incident is shown in Truffaut's *Les Quatre Cents Coups (The 400 Blows)*.

François is at a school holiday camp when he writes to Robert.

To Robert Lachenay

(Binic, 1945)

My dear Robert,

I was really pleased to receive your two packages. Balzac has arrived safely. Don't send me any more magazines since I'll have to pay about 80F in postage to send it all back to you. I went to the post office with the empty box. My father is to send me 200 francs out of which there will be 80F for postage + 60F for the movies which I owe the headmaster that makes 140 francs.

Things are lousy and I mean really lousy! We went to see *A Thousand and One Nights*! It's better than *The Thief of Bagdad* but nothing to write home about. Just reading your cinema magazines makes me want to be in Paris as there seem to me lots of good films. Edward Robinson is all the rage at the moment since he's acting in 3 new films! I hope my letter won't find you still wishing it were last year. Should I send the magazines back to you at Le

Tréport or in Paris? Try to be careful when bathing ~~on the rails~~ (it was a chum who wrote that).

I have to go as the peeryod of skoolwurk iz finnysht.

Lotz a luv,

Phronssouas your chumm.

Discuss in your next letter my nocturnal and subterranean odyssey in the Métro the cause, the action, its consequence, discuss how it happened that I slept in the Métro when we were at Ducornet's. Because my chums refuse to believe me.

GROUCHO MARX (1890–1977)

comedian

Groucho (Julius Henry) Marx was the middle one of the five Marx brothers. They were all born in New York and died in Los Angeles. Their father was a poor Jewish tailor of Alsatian descent, their mother had been on the stage. She lost no time in training their five boys to follow in her footsteps, and three of them, Groucho, Harpo and Chico, became major film stars. In later life, Groucho, the survivor, continued as a professional comedian and television personality. He also published *The Groucho Letters*.

Groucho replies to Marjorie Nedford, aged eleven, who had written to him, 'My father met your brother Gummo here in Palm Springs, and he said if I write to you, he was sure you would send me an autograph . . .'

January 15, 1947

Dear Marjorie,

I think you should warn your father about this man Gummo. For years he has palmed himself off as one of the Marx Brothers and has made a good thing of it. Actually he is no more one of the Marx Brothers than Chico is one of the Dolly Sisters.

Confidentially, this Gummo comes from a long line of Rumanian Gypsies; he was deposited at our doorstep at the age of fifty, and there's nothing we can do about it.

Here is the autograph. I would send you a lock of my hair but it's at the barbershop getting washed.

Sincerely,
Groucho Marx

He writes to Sylvia Sheekman, his accountant's daughter.

January 3, 1949

Dear Sylvia

I finally finished the gingerbread man. I didn't mean to eat him, but it was either him or me. The last thing I ate was his foot and this I didn't expect. Sylvia, you won't believe this but on the way down my gullet he kicked me. This is a fine world we are living in when you can't even trust a gingerbread man.

I hope you have a very happy 1949 and that you are laying in a good supply of ginger for next Christmas.

Yours Pseudo-uncle
Groucho

C.S. LEWIS (1898–1963)
literary critic and novelist

Clive Staples ('Jack') Lewis was an academic who became widely known for his Christian writings (e.g. *The Screwtape Letters*), his science fiction (*Out of the Silent Planet*, etc.) and the Narnia Chronicles for children. As a result of Narnia vast numbers of children wrote to him from all over the world, notably America. To one young correspondent he wrote, 'the funny thing is that I was far worse about writing letters when I had far fewer to write; now that I have such a lot to write I've just got to do them all at once, first thing every morning'.

TO A FIFTH-GRADE CLASS IN MARYLAND

May 29th, 1954

Dear Fifth Graders

. . .

I'm tall, fat, rather bald, red-faced, double-chinned, black-haired, have a deep voice, and wear glasses for reading.

. . .

TO HILA

June 3rd, 1953

Dear [Hila]

Thank you so much for your lovely letter and pictures. I realised at once that the coloured one was not a particular scene but a sort of line-up like what you would have at the very end if it was a play instead of stories. *The*

[Voyage of the] 'Dawn Treader' is *not* to be the last: There are to be 4 more, 7 in all. Didn't you notice that Aslan said nothing about Eustace not going back? I thought the best of your pictures was the one of Mr. Tumnus at the bottom of the letter. As to Aslan's other name, well I want you to guess. Has there never been anyone in *this* world who (1.) Arrived at the same time as Father Christmas. (2.) Said he was the son of the Great Emperor. (3.) Gave himself up for someone else's fault to be jeered at and killed by wicked people. (4.) Came to life again. (5.) Is sometimes spoken of as a Lamb (see the end of the Dawn Treader). Don't you really know his name in this world. Think it over and let me know your answer!

Reepicheep in your coloured picture has just the right perky, cheeky expression. I love real mice. There are lots in my room in College but I have never set a trap. When I sit up late working they poke their heads out from behind the curtains just as if they were saying, 'Hi! Time for *you* to go to bed. We want to come out and play.'

All good wishes,
Yours ever
C.S. Lewis

TO PHYLLIDA

14th Sept 1953

Dear Phyllida

Although your letter was written a month ago I only got it to-day, for I have been away in Donegal [Republic of Ireland], (which is glorious). Thanks v.[ery] much: it is so interesting to hear exactly what people do like and don't like, which is just what grown-up readers never really tell.

Now about *kids*. I also hate the word. But if you mean the place in *P.[rince] Caspian* chap 8, the point is that Edmund hated it too. He was using the rottenest word just because it *was* the rottenest word, running himself down as much as possible, because he was making a fool of the Dwarf – as you might say 'of course I can only *strum*' when you really knew you could play the piano quite as well as the other person. But if I have used *kids* anywhere else (I hope I haven't) then I'm sorry: you are quite right in objecting to it. And you are also right about the party turned into stone in the woods. I thought people would take it for granted that Aslan would put it all right. But I see now that I should have said so.

By the way, do you think the Dark Island is *too* frightening for small children? Did it give your brother the horrors? I was nervous about that, but I left it in because I thought one can never be sure what will or will not frighten people.

There are to be 7 Narnian stories altogether. I am sorry they are so dear: it is the publisher, not me, who fixes the price. Here is the new one. [*The Silver Chair*].

As I say, I think *you* are right about the other points but I feel sure I'm right to make them grow up in Narnia. Of course they will grow up in this world too. You'll see. You see, I don't think age matters so much as people think. Parts of me are still 12 and I think other parts were already 50 when I was 12: so I don't feel it v.[ery] odd that they grow up in Narnia when they are children in England.

yours sincerely
C.S. Lewis

[19 September 1953]

Dear Phyllida,

I feel as one does when *after* 'showing up' one's work one realises one has made the very same mistake one got into a row for last week! I mean, *after* sending off the book, I read it myself and 'kids' again twice. I really will take care not to do it again . . .

TO JOAN

The Kilns
Headington Quarry
Oxford
[26 June 1956]

Dear Joan –

Thank you for your letter of the 3rd. You describe your Wonderful Night v.[ery] well. That is, you describe the place and the people and the night and the feeling of it all, very well – but not the *thing* itself – the setting but not the jewel. And no wonder! Wordsworth often does just the same. His *Prelude* (you're bound to read it about 10 years hence. Don't try it now, or you'll only spoil it for later reading) is full of moments in which everything except the *thing* itself is described. If you become a writer you'll be trying to describe the *thing* all your life: and lucky if, out of dozens of books, one or two sentences, just for a moment, come near to getting it across.

About *amn't, aren't I* and *am I not*, of course there are no right or wrong answers about language in the sense in which there are right and wrong answers in Arithmetic. 'Good English' is whatever educated people talk; so that what is good in one place or time w[oul]d not be so in another. *Amn't I* was good 50 years ago in the North of Ireland where I was brought up, but bad in Southern England. *Aren't I* w[oul]d have been hideously bad in Ireland but very good in England. And of course I just don't know which (if either) is good in modern Florida. Don't take any notice of teachers and textbooks in such matters. Nor of logic. It is good to say 'more than one passenger was hurt,' although *more than one* equals at least two and therefore logically the verb ought to be plural *were* not singular *was*!

What really matters is: –

1. Always try to use the language so as to make quite clear what you mean and make sure y[ou]r sentence couldn't mean anything else.

2. Always prefer the plain direct word to the long, vague one. Don't *implement* promises, but *keep* them.

3. Never use abstract nouns when concrete ones will do. If you mean 'More people died' don't say 'Mortality rose'.

4. In writing. Don't use adjectives which merely tell us how you want us to *feel* about the thing you are describing. I mean, instead of telling us a thing was 'terrible,' describe it so that we'll be terrified. Don't say it was 'delightful'; make *us* say 'delightful' when we've read the description. You see, all those words (horrifying, wonderful, hideous, exquisite) are only like saying to your readers 'Please will you do my job for me.'

5. Don't use words too big for the subject. Don't say 'infinitely' when you mean 'very'; otherwise you'll have no word left when you want to talk about something *really* infinite.

Thanks for the photos. You and Aslan both look v[ery] well. I hope you'll like your new home.

With love
yours
C.S. Lewis

EVELYN WAUGH (1903–1966)

novelist

Evelyn Waugh had seven children, six of whom survived, by his second wife, Laura. They were: Teresa, Auberon, Margaret, Harriet, James and Septimus, all born between 1938 and 1950. They were all sent away to school at an early age.

Waugh's diaries include several tartly critical entries about his offspring. 'The presence of my children fills me with deep weariness and depression'; 'I found the company exceedingly irksome and the holidays dragged on'; 'I used to take some pleasure in inventing legends for them about Basil Bennett, Dr Bedlam and the Sebag-Montefiores but now they think it ingenuous to squeal 'it isn't true', and 'I find the children particularly charmless'.

Nevertheless, he is conscientious. He and Laura take notice when, in 1953, Margaret's letters become 'piteous', look into things and transfer her and Harriet to another school. And when Bron runs into trouble at Downside, Waugh plays his parental part and writes, from Jamaica:

27 January 1955

Dear Bron,

I was sorry not to see you before your return to Downside. Had I done so I would have offered you some sage advice. I got the impression that last term you were going a bit far in your defiance of school rules. I should hate you to be low-spirited and submissive, but don't become an anarchist. Don't above all things put on side. It is an excellent thing to see through the side of others – particularly youths who think they are young Gods because they are good at games. But they at least are good at something. There is no superiority in shirking things and doing things badly. Be superior by cultivating your intellect and your taste. Enough of this, but pay attention to it . . .

The trouble continues, and he answers a letter from Bron, rather more bluntly:

                                        Piers Court
                                        23 May 1955

My dear Bron,

Dont write in that silly tone. No one has any motive with regard to you except your own welfare. No decision is absolute yet. If you have a better suggestion to make I shall be glad to hear it.

I warned you at the beginning of last term that you were heading for trouble. You paid no attention. I need not repeat what I said to you at the end of this holidays. I could not tell you then what I had in mind for your future, as I had left the Headmaster to make his own arrangements in his own time with the house-masters. I fully realise that it is a most unusual kindness of the Headmaster's to allow you to change houses. My first idea was to send you to another school. It is possible that Stonyhurst might take you, but I should have to ask them to do so as a favour, and I cannot do this unless I am confident that you intend to behave yourself. If you go there as Psmith and Mike went to Sedleigh, determined to sulk, it would be hopeless.

You have made a mess of things. At your age that is not a disaster, but you must help yourself. Your future, temporal and spiritual, is your own making. I can only provide opportunities for your achievements.

                        Your affectionate papa
                        E.W.

Waugh has just had to send a stiff letter to his son Auberon. But three weeks later he is very ready to praise where praise is due.

Piers Court
14 June 1955

My dear Bron,—I congratulate you with all my heart on your success with
your story. You do not name the discerning magazine – *Everybody's* perhaps?
[No: *Lilliput.*] Anyway it is an agreeable thing to see one's work
professionally recognized. I look forward greatly to seeing the issue. They
won't pay you until the end of the month in which it appears. That is the
usual practice.

Your hairless Uncle Alec Waugh has also had a success at last. His latest
book [*Island in the Sun*] has been taken by the American 'Book of the
Month', serialized, filmed – in fact the jack-pot. It is very nice for him after
so many years of disappointment, obscurity. He has not drawn a sober
breath since he heard the news . . .

I am glad the Headmaster is paying attention to you. His aim, I think, is
to find whether it is better to continue your education or to send you with a
changed name and £5 to Australia . . .

Your affec. papa
E.W.

In the hope of understanding Bron better he reads the diaries he
himself kept at his son's age. 'I was appalled at their vulgarity and prig-
gishness.' Waugh is a practising Catholic: he prays for tolerance and
kindness in his dealings with the boy, virtues not always vouchsafed to
him.

Margaret wins her father's approval. He takes her to Paris, and awards
her five top adjectives for the ideal travelling companion: 'She was
sunny, intelligent, tireless, affectionate, polite.' In the same year Teresa
was a debutante. He describes the scene to Margaret:

Piers Court
17 March [1956]

Darling Meg,

I went to London to take Teresa to a debutantes' cocktail party given by a friend of mine. There were 250 pimply youths and 250 hideous girls packed so tight together they could not move hand or foot. So I sat with the butler in the hall and that is the last anyone has seen of Teresa. I suppose she was crushed to death & the corpse too flat to be recognised. About 100 dead girls were carried out & buried in a common pit. R.I.P. I shall never let you, my ewe lamb, become a debutante . . .

When it comes to Teresa's own ball there is an equally inventive account to sisters Margaret and Harriet.

Piers Court
8 July [1956]

Darling Meg & Hatty,

It is very vulgar of you (Meg) to want to see press cuttings about your sister's ball. We kept out photographers, of course, and tried to keep out journalists but some nasty guest must have gossiped and there were some silly paragraphs in one or two of the commoner papers.

However it was a great success. Teresa wore a dress of emerald green calico trimmed with zebra skin and a straw hat, button boots of patent leather and woollen gloves & was greatly admired. Unfortunately she was given a black eye by Alice Jolliffe but we bandaged her up & she managed well with one eye.

We had the Stinchcombe Silvular Band to play and Miss Mildmay crooned. For supper there was plenty of stout and kippers and bread & margarine and blancmange and plum jam for those who came early but it soon ran out.

Your mother insisted on bringing all 14 cows and they took up most of the ballroom but there was a little tent in the garden. Christina McDonnell and Susan Baring smoked clay pipes all the time & the tent grew rather stuffy. A lot of criminals came uninvited and began robbing everyone so the police charged with truncheons and, I am sorry to say, arrested Alec Waugh and Alick Dru by mistake. They are still in prison but we hope to get them out on bail in a day or two. To make things difficult Alick Dru had five watches, six diamond rings and some silver spoons in his pocket when arrested so he may get sent to prison for a year or two.

One of the cows escaped from the ball room into the Kensington Square Convent. The nuns have been milking her ever since & feeding her on sunflower seeds.

Polly Grant was murdered by a black man whom your Uncle Auberon brought. Otherwise the ball was a great success.

Your affec. papa
E.W.

Margaret also has trouble at school and asks to leave early. Waugh at first cautions against this.

Combe Florey House
3 June [1957]

Darling Meg

A sad and saddening letter from you. I am so sorry you are in hot water. You do not have to tell me that you have not done anything really wicked. I know my pig. I am absolutely confident that you will never never be dishonourable, impure or cruel. That is all that matters.

I think it is a weakness of girls' schools that they have no adequate punishments. When a boy is naughty he is beaten and that is the end of it. All this admonition makes for resentment and the part of your letter that I don't like at all is where you say the nuns 'hate' you. That is rubbish. And when you run down girls who behave better than you. That is mean. Chuck it, Meg.

It is only three weeks since Mother Bridget was writing warmly of your 'great efforts' to reconcile yourself to school. If you have lapsed in the meantime it is only a naughty mood. Don't whine about it.

As to your leaving early – we can discuss that next holidays. I was miserable at Lancing and kept asking my father to take me away, I am very glad now that he did not. The same with Bron. The whole of our life is a test & a preparation for heaven – most of it irksome. So each part of our life is an irksome test & preparation for something better. I think you would greatly enjoy Oxford and get the best out of it. But you can't get there without much boring labour and discipline.

Don't get into your silly head the idea that anyone hates you or is unfair to you. You are loved far beyond your deserts, especially by your

Papa

Less than a week later Margaret receives this letter from her father and she leaves the school at the end of the term.

Combe Florey House

7 June [1957]

Darling Meg,

I send you all my love for your birthday. I hope it is a very happy day despite the persecution of Mother Bridget.

You have certainly made a resourceful & implacable enemy in that holy lady. She has written both to Colonel Batchelor and Mrs. Critchley-Salmonson[1] strong denunciations of your moral character and behaviour. I have sent these documents to my solicitors and hope you will soon appear in the courts suing her for libel. Damages will be so heavy that no doubt the school will have to close down.

She has done more than that. She has written to the committee of the St. James's Club warning them not to admit you to luncheon on 23rd. I have

---

[1] Colonel Batchelor and his sister Mrs Critchley-Salmonson were the previous owners of Combe Florey.

had a letter from the Chairman asking whether it is true that you steal the silver when asked to come to luncheon. She also told them that you are invariably drunk & disorderly. I call that a bit thick.

But her most cruel move has been to circulate all the London fishmongers warning them under pain of mortal sin not to have any whitebait during your visit to London. The poor men are so frightened of her that they have forbidden the fishermen to catch any for the next fortnight.

Her powers are infinite. She has agents everywhere. I fear you have got yourself into an appalling predicament.

I have just received a letter from Lady Diana [Cooper] who writes: 'Since learning from Mother Bridget of Margaret's terrible wickedness I wish you to destroy the photograph of her and me which was taken last year. I do not want there to be any evidence of my ever having met the odious girl.'

All this malevolent campaign must, I am afraid, rather over-cloud your birthday. Nevertheless I hope you have some pleasure in eating the cakes which, I know, the other girls will refuse to share with you.

Sweet Meg, don't be a donkey. Everyone loves you – particularly I – me? Which I wonder is grammatical.

Your loving
Papa

JOYCE CARY (1888–1957)

novelist

Joyce Cary was born in Londonderry but educated in England. He joined the colonial administration, but by 1920 had settled in England with a full-time writing career. He writes to Sarah Fischer (aged twelve), who was the daughter of friends Cary had made in the USA. When he was near to dying of cancer, and his voice was very faint, Sarah wrote to him with a suggestion that whistling Morse Code might be helpful. He replied:

February 12, 1957

My dear Sarah,

Thank you so much for your letter and its very good suggestion. The only thing is that now the laryngitis has cleared up it has been discovered that my trouble is weakness of the diaphragm, which produces breathlessness and difficulty in my speech, so I am afraid whistling would be just as difficult as speaking, but Morse Code might certainly help communication.

I am so glad you are enjoying life as you grow up. In my experience, life is much more fun when you do grow up.

Ever yours affectionately,

My love to you, my dear

Joyce Cary

Cary often joked as death drew nearer, relishing a conversation with his little grandson who speculated matter-of-factly, 'I shouldn't think you'll last much longer . . .' The magnificent end to *The Horse's Mouth* comes to mind. Gulley Jimpson is in hospital. A nursing nun sits by his bed.

"'Please don't talk', said the nun . . . 'It's dangerous for you to talk, you're very seriously ill.' 'Not so seriously as you're well. How you don't enjoy life, mother. I should laugh all round my neck at this minute if my shirt wasn't a bit on the tight side.' 'It would be better for you to pray.' 'Same thing, mother'".

JAMES THURBER (1894–1961)
American writer and cartoonist

James Thurber was born in Columbus, Ohio. His idiosyncratic vein of humour was expressed with equal facility in both words and pictures. It touched genius when a caption perfectly matched a drawing.

Thurber wrote a semi-autobiographical account of his experiences as a regular contributor to the *New Yorker*, *The Years with Ross*; produced several volumes of essays and short stories; collaborated with E.B. White on *Is Sex Necessary?* and, in 1947, when he was almost blind his story, *The Secret Life of Walter Mitty* was successfully filmed, starring Danny Kaye.

The following letter was anthologized in *Mr Thurber Regrets*, (1947).

West Cornwall
Connecticut

Mr. Robert Leifert
New York City, New York

January 4, 1958

Dear Robert:

Since a hundred schoolchildren a year write me letters like yours – some writers get a thousand – the problem of what to do about such classroom 'projects' has become a serious one for all of us. If a writer answered all of you he would get nothing else done. When I was a baby goat I had to do my own research on projects, and I enjoyed doing it. I never wrote an author for his autograph or photograph in my life. Photographs are for movie actors to send to girls. Tell your teacher I said so, and please send me her name . . .

One of the things that discourage us writers is the fact that 90 percent of you children write wholly, or partly, illiterate letters, carelessly typed. You yourself write 'clarr' for 'class' and that's a honey, Robert, since *s* is next to *a*, and *r* is on the line above. Most schoolchildren in America would do a dedication like the following (please find the mistakes in it and write me about them):

> *To Miss Effa G. Burns*
> *Without who's help*
> *this book could never*
> *of been finished,*
> *is dedicated with*
> *gartitude by it's*
> *arthur.*

Show that to your teacher and tell her to show it to her principal, and see if they can find the mistakes . . .

Just yesterday a letter came in from a girl your age in South Carolina asking for biographical material and photograph. That is not the kind of education they have in Russia, we are told, because it's too much like a hobby or waste of time. What do you and your classmates want to be when you grow up – collectors? Then who is going to help keep the United States ahead of Russia in science, engineering, and the arts?

Please answer this letter. If you don't I'll write to another pupil.

> *Sincerely yours,*
> James Thurber

ROBERT LUTYENS (1901–72)

architect, designer, artist

The son of Sir Edwin Lutyens, Robert Lutyens showed no signs in his youth of achieving the status so fervently yearned for by his famous father. He was sent down from Cambridge and married, when she was nineteen, the Polish-born niece of Chaim Weizmann, Eva Lubrujinska. She was related to the Sieff family which was how, after a spell as art editor of the *Daily Mail*, he became designer of the façades for Marks & Spencer. Later, reconciled with his father, they collaborated on country houses, including Middleton Park. A second marriage, after World War II, took him to America for about a decade, but in 1959, back in Britain, he married Joan May and they had a daughter, Candia, to whom the letter below was written. She does not remember reading it thoroughly until some three years after his death.

Postscript for Candia
March 1968

I

Come to me in my dreams and then
By day I shall be well again . . .

This is an invocation to you – to me may be so!

You have asked me to write to you a whole book about the old-fashioned times, and about the future. Quite a tall order!

In my old age (my darling) I have forgotten too many of the differentiations that made life beautiful. So what shall I impart to you? Not wisdom, for that you will acquire. Not experience, since I have profited from so little of it myself. Not recollections that are too remote to be of any concern to you, and which lack cogency if the events commemorated were not shared. It may be true to say that nothing that isn't shared is worth-while having: and this is possibly the clue to all living – to living backwards in recollection, to living forward in expectation, from living to day to day in tenderness and solicitude. We have at least shared almost every moment of your life to date.

I cannot bring to you the echo of old songs, which make my pulse beat faster when I hear their litany repeated at odd moments on the telly. There is no purpose in telling you that I saw Leonora Duse on the stage, or Nijinski dance; that I knew Pepita's daughter, and used to walk with my father down Bond Street on a summer morning following the delicious scent of a coal cart, to have breakfast in St. James's Square, before motor-cars had made existence horrible.

On the other hand I can tell you quite a lot about yourself; and since you are unlikely to know it from any other source, I feel it a sort of duty to fill in some of the facts in the story of your heritage.

But all I can really write for you is something in the nature of an apology to the 60 years difference in our ages. I shall have to desert you sooner than you would normally have reason to expect, on the other hand, next year – in March 1969 – is the centenary of your grandfather's birth; and this of course gives you an unusual place in the span of contemporary history; and you should at least know your place in it.

There is a quotation the source of which I can't remember, nor can I quote it accurately. But it goes something like this; 'The loss of the child deprives the parent of the future. The loss of the parent deprives the child of the past.'

There may come a time later on when you may find yourself in need of establishing your identity. The necessity never arose in my own case and in that of my sister's, because we were surrounded by such a host of relatives and acquaintances, that our identity was literally forced upon us.

You see, the civilized world has possibly changed more in the 67 years of my life than during any time that ever proceeded it. The changes that appear to me are of course superficial and it is the superficial changes that I am concerned with. The changes are in fact profound; and at the moment it looks as though the human race is proving to be a success in as much as it is multiplying. There is no other test; although failure may be implicit in its inability to deal with the problems of expansion.

My old friend, Stanley Morison, who died last year and who came to embrace the bleak, hopeless pessimism of the Roman Catholic faith, used to proclaim that nothing had improved since the Garden of Eden except the plumbing.

I don't believe that to be true; or rather let it be said that I have more confidence in w.c.'s than in R.C.'s! Nevertheless, the whole of history is a record of the achievements of the few at the expense of the many. Culture – the attainment of human excellence – has hitherto been the product of the surplus; and as it says in the Apocrypha, 'Wisdom cometh by opportunity of leisure.' It is what is called privilege; and whether one approves of it or not I was born to privilege and, although to a limited extent, you were born to it too. There is nothing admirable about it. It is a fact. And because it is just a fact there is nothing shameful about it either, unless it be held to my account that I have never succeeded in taking much advantage of it. Your progenitors were relatively privileged people; and if some of them had exceptional talent as well it is merely incidental to the story. Anyhow, my only purpose in writing is to try and make the story coherent for you, and to bring it up to date.

This engaging letter covers some thirty pages of manuscript. The recipient, now Candia Petersen, founded a company that reproduces furniture designed by her father and grandfather.

KENNETH TYNAN (1927–1980)

dramatic critic

Ken Tynan was the influential dramatic critic of the London *Observer* in the 1950s, and champion of John Osborne and Bertolt Brecht particularly. As Literary Manager of the National Theatre from its foundation until 1973, he worked closely with Sir Laurence Olivier to formulate policy and select plays, often meeting intense opposition from the board of governors. He wrote and co-produced *Oh, Calcutta!*, an erotic revue which could not have been performed publicly while stage censorship, of which he was a fierce opponent, lasted.

His first wife was Elaine Dundy, the novelist: they had one daughter, Tracy. His second was the Canadian-born journalist Kathleen Halton. They had two children, Roxana and Matthew, to whom Tynan wrote the birthday verses reprinted below. He died of emphysema in Santa Monica, USA. Kathleen Tynan wrote his life (1987) and edited his letters (1994).

[20 Thurloe Square]
14 September 1976
Roxana's 9th Birthday by Ken
For Roxana at Nine

Lift the glasses! Pour the wine!
Dear Roxana, you are nine!
There was much to celebrate
When you reached the age of eight;
And two years ago, by heaven,
How we cheered when you were seven!

And a man with magic tricks
Made you laugh when you were six.
'May you prosper! May you thrive!'
Was my wish when you were five;
And the same was true at four
(Sorry if I sound a bore);
While the day that you were three
Friends and neighbours roared with glee.
When the candles numbered two,
Mummy cried (and Daddy, too);
And there never was more fun
Than on birthday number one
(Not since that September morn
When stars danced and you were born).
Still for nine I'll do my best.
Joy I wish you, health and rest.
Happy work to useful ends,
And a few beloved friends;
Just the right amount of money
And a sense of what is funny;
Grace and courage when you're pressed,
And each day a good night's rest.
Sunshine and blue skies attend you
All these gifts I'd like to send you,
As befits a girl of nine
Who is pretty, wise and mine.
(In return I ask for this;
Give me now and then a kiss;
Learn the language used in France;
And – above all – learn to dance.)

[9454 Lloydcrest Drive
Beverly Hills Cal. 90210]
14 September 1978

To Roxana at Eleven

Lift your glasses high as Heaven –
Miss Roxana is eleven!
Bright as button, gay as bee,
Most nice things a girl should be:
Pretty as a pot of paint,
She says 'isn't', never 'ain't';
Works with dedicated zeal,
Dives as sleekly as a seal;
Yes, I wouldn't be surprised
If she grew up civilised.
. . .
Now, like every other daughter
Of her age, she's on the border –
Leaving childhood's nursery
For the realms of puberty,
Where the shadows seem much longer
But the sunlight is far stronger.
. . .
All I wish you, darling Rox,
From a little magic box,
Is the poise of a Rolls-Royce
And the wit of Hepburn's voice,
Plus the vision of King Arthur
And the wisdom of Siddhartha
(Which, you'll find, is anudder
Name for him we call the Buddha):
And the valour of Saint Joan,
Serving gods that are your own,
(Don't stare always at the steeple –
Look inside and serve the people);
Next, though you may think this is silly,
Be as loonie as Bea Lillie
(Which, as I'll explain to you,

Is quite difficult to do),
And, unless it's too much bother,
Be as loving as your mother.
Lastly: show compassion,
Even to a baddie –
Never kick sand
Upon your loving Daddy.
XXX
XXX
XXX
XX

This is the last letter, set down in a shaky hand, that Kenneth
Tynan wrote. He died in St John's Hospital, Santa Monica, on 26 July
1980.

[15 Stone Canyon Road]
9 June 1980

Dear Matthew, dear boy,
Relax and enjoy
The day of your birth.
Start your tenth year on earth
With a wild jungle yell
And a kiss from Michelle.

When you were seven
Your idea of heaven
Was being a whizz at karate,
Then you were eight,
And you thought it was great
To stay out all night at a party.

Now that you're nine,
I'm sure you'll be fine
Funny, and fine, and clever –
And I send you my love forever.

Daddy
June 1980

ARTHUR ASHE (1945–1993)

American tennis player

Ashe was the first black tennis player to join the American Davis Cup team, and the first to win the Wimbledon men's singles final (1975). He was a policeman's son, brought up in Richmond, Virginia, when that state still practised segregation.

In 1977 Ashe married Jeanne Moutassamy. Four years later he underwent a quadruple heart by-pass operation. Jeanne's family also had a history of heart disease, despite which, with doctor's advice, they decided to have a child, and Camera Elizabeth was born in 1986. Two years later, following brain surgery, Ashe was discovered to be HIV positive. This was traced to a second heart operation and an infected transfusion of blood. He died in 1993.

During the last months of his life, having set up foundations to help impoverished inner cities, and to defeat AIDS, he wrote *Days of Grace*, setting down his personal philosophy. It includes a letter to his daughter, extracts from which appear below, and another letter to Camera, published in *The Times* of 28 June 1993 from the sports writer, David Miller, who wrote a thrilling description of the 1975 final. The editor would like to have included it here but Rupert Murdoch's terms were too onerous.

ARTHUR ASHE TO CAMERA

My dear Camera,

By the time you read this letter from me to you for the first time, I may not be around to discuss with you what I have written here. Perhaps I will still be with you and your mother, sharing in your daily lives, in your joys and in your sorrows. However, I may be gone. You would doubtless be sad that I am gone, and remember me clearly for a while. Then I will exist only as a memory already beginning to fade in your mind. Although it is natural for memories to fade, I am writing this letter in the hope that your recollection of me will never fade completely. I would like to remain a part of your life, Camera, for as long as you live.

I was only a few months older than you are now when I lost my own mother. Eventually I had no memory of what she was actually like, how her voice sounded, how her touch felt. I wanted desperately to know these things, but she was gone and I could not recover that knowledge. For your sake, as well as mine, I hope that I am around for a long time. But we cannot always have what we want, and we must prepare for and accept those changes over which we have no control.

Coincidentally, Camera, I am writing this letter to you on the same day as the inauguration in Washington, D.C. – January 20, 1993, – just a few hours after William Jefferson Clinton became the new president of the United States of America . . . I especially loved listening to Maya Angelou, tall and dignified with a rich melodious voice, read the poem that our new president asked her to write especially for this occasion . . . She spoke of 'a rock, a river, a tree' . . . For me, the river and the tree hold special significance as symbols because they are so much part of African American folklore and history, as religion and culture in the South where I was born and grew up, and where so many other black folk have lived in slavery and freedom . . .

Rivers flows forever and ever changing. At no two moments in time is a river the same. The water in the river is always changing. Life is like that . . .

What is sure to be different for you will be the quickening pace of change as you grow older. Believe me, most people resist change, even when it promises to be for the better. But change will come, and if you acknowledge this simple but indisputable fact, then you will have a head start. I want you to use that advantage, to become a leader among people . . .

On the other hand, Camera, certain things do not change. They are immutable. Maya Angelou's tree stands for family, both immediate and extended. She had in mind, I imagine, some towering, leafy oak, with massive and deep roots that allow the tree to bend in the fiercest wind and yet survive . . . Families that survive are like that tree . . .

You must be like that, too, Camera, although your fighting must always be for morally justifiable ends. You are part of a tree. On Grandpa's – my father's – side of our family, we proudly display our family tree carefully painted by Grandpa's cousin Thelma . . . Your name, Camera Elizabeth

Ashe, is one of the freshest leaves on this old tree. You are the daughter of a tenth-generation African American. You must never forget your place on that tree . . .

Arthur Ashe then describes his wife's family history and gives Camera advice on marriage. He urges her to find friendship amongst all colours and creeds, exhorts her to learn other languages, look after her health, develop a feeling for art, music, poetry, and, above all, to have faith in God.

Finally . . .

I end, Camera, as I began, with family. In nearly every civilization of which I have heard, the family is the central social unit, the base and foundation of the culture . . .

I may not be walking with you all the way, or even much of the way, as I walk with you now. Don't be angry with me if I am not there in person, alive and well, when you need me. I would like nothing more than to be with you always. Do not feel sorry for me if I am gone. When we were together, I loved you deeply and you gave me so much happiness I can never repay you. Camera, wherever I am when you take down this book and read in it, or when you stumble and fall and don't know if you can get up again, think of me. I will be watching and smiling and cheering you on.

MAVIS NORRIE (b. 1926)

a contemporary grandmother

whose details are on the dust jacket of this book, writes a picture-book letter to her four grandchildren, with pictures kindly drawn by

MICHAEL FLOYD (1923–1997)

artist, architect

Michael Floyd (illustrator) met his wife, Pat, while both were in the RAF in World War II. They found that each of them had studied architecture. Subsequently they worked together in an architectural practice. Of all their projects, they liked best those involving hospitals. They had nine grandchildren.

In retirement Michael never stopped drawing, just as the Grandpa in the story is an ex-bookseller who never stops writing (except when he is looking after Grandma). Recently he and Michael collaborated on three books on France and Italy.

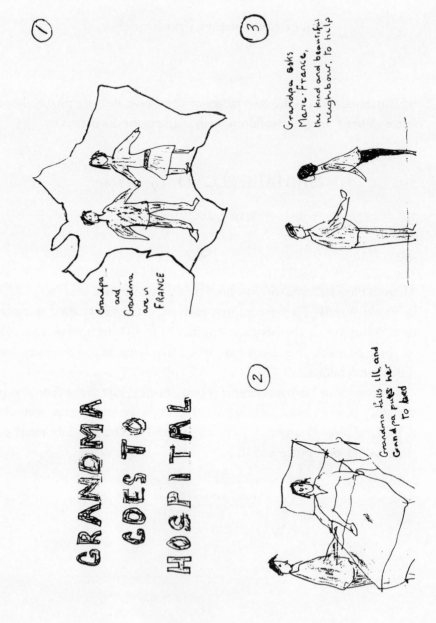

① Grandpa and Grandma are in FRANCE

GRANDMA GOES TO HOSPITAL

② Grandma falls ill, and Grandpa puts her to bed

③ Grandpa asks Marie-France, the kind and beautiful neighbour, to help

④

Marie-France calls the doctor. He is a big man with a big voice. He says:

"THIS GRANDMA MUST GO TO HOSPITAL!"

⑤

The ambulance arrives

Two ambulance men put Grandma on the stretcher and then put her in the ambulance.

⑥

It is a tiny ambulance for one person only. Grandpa and Marie-France follow in the big red car.

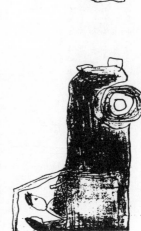

(Marie-France always accompanies Grandma to hospital.)

⑦

At the hospital doctors and nurses examine Grandma. They say:

"This Grandma is not sweet enough! She must be sweetened!"

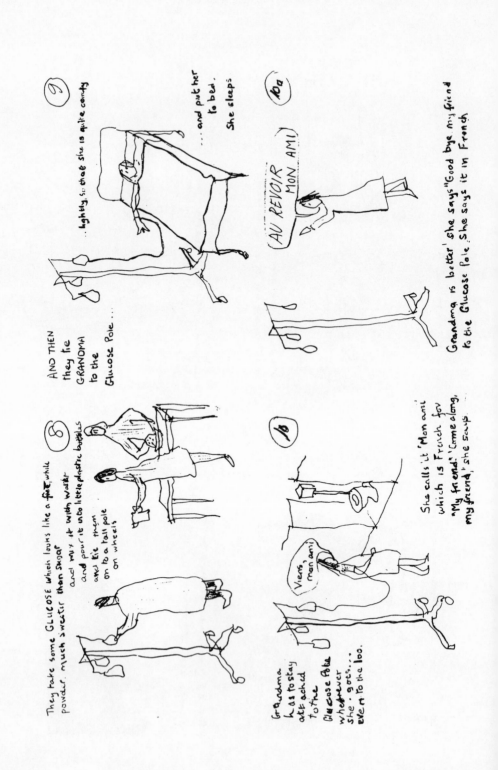

But what's this??!!! Grandma is getting smaller and thinner and all bent over!

11

11/a

So Grandpa comes and takes Grandma —home in the big red car......

12

HÔPITAL

GRANDMA HAS NOT BEEN EATING HER HOSPITAL DINNERS

13

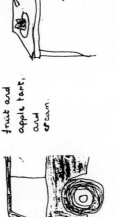

...and feeds her on smoked salmon and chicken and crisp lettuce and fruit and apple tart, and cream

Miam! miam!

"Yum yum" she says - in French

GRANDMA GOES TO HOSPITAL

Written by Grandma
drawn by Michael Floyd

The Grandpa and Grandma Press 1994.

Other publications
by the
Grandpa and Grandma Press

Grandpa and Grandma go to France. 1992   1 copy
written by Grandma, drawn by Grandpa
Grandpa and Grandma on holiday. 1993.   1 copy
written by Grandma, drawn by Grandpa
Coming Soon: Grandpa and Grandma move house
written by Grandma, drawn by Grandpa

...and now
Grandma is
quite well again
and Grandpa
is not on his own
any more

(14)

JOAN AIKEN, (1924–   )

author

Joan Aiken, daughter of Conrad (qv p. 189) and great-granddaughter of Elizabeth Aiken (qv p. 133), is a prolific writer of children's stories, thrillers and Jane Austen reconstructions. This letter to her daughter was written when Liz (Brown) was already 17, perhaps 18, and therefore does not officially qualify for inclusion here. I have kept my rule until the very end of the book and make this exception only because this letter seems to encapsulate the attitudes common to loving parents at the end of the twentieth century.

Dear Liz

You can do whatever you want to with your life, because I know you can find your own way to be happy. The last thing that should worry you is whether I approve or not. Frankly, sometimes I don't! But I love you and I think your self-confidence and success with yourself depend on knowing that you are free, so I want to tell you that once and for all. I love you very much and I look forward to seeing you, whenever you come.

Much love from Ma.

P.S. I shall make sure not to be at all busy when you come.

P.S. This is all true!

SOURCES

page

xvii *Swing hammer swing!* by Jeff Torrington, Secker & Warburg, 1993.

1 Translated from the original Latin in *Epigrammata clarissimi disertissimique uiri Thomae Mori Britanni ad emendatum exemplar ipsius autoris excussa. Apud Inclytam Basileam. Basileae apud Ioannem Frobenium mense Decembri Anno MDXX,* p. 110.

4 *Martin Luther* by A. McGiffery, New York, 1911

6 *Letters of Queen Elizabeth,* ed. G.B. Harrison, Cassell, 1938

9 *A Collection of the works of William Penn,* London, 1726

11 *Lord Chesterfield's Letters,* ed. D. Roberts, O.U.P, 1992

17 *The Works of Laurence Sterne,* Volume the Ninth, London, 1798

19 *The Letters of Charles Burney,* ed. Ribero, O.U.P., 1991

22 *Marie Antoinette* by Stefan Zweig, Cassell, 1933

24 From *Mrs Chapone's Letters, Dr Gregory's Legacy, and Lady Pennington's Advice,* J. Walker & Edwards, Paternoster Row, London, 1774

26 *The Family Letters of Thomas Jefferson,* University Press of Virginia, 1986

30 *Letters to Children by Eva G. Connor,* Macmillan, New York, 1938

32 *Beloved Emma* by Flora Fraser, Weidenfeld & Nicolson, 1986: *Life & Letters of Emma Hamilton,* H. Tours, Gollancz, 1963

32 *A Portrait of Lord Nelson,* by Oliver Warner, Pelican Books, 1963

37 *The Browning Correspondence, 1809–1842,* ed. Kelley & Hudson, Wedgestone Press, USA

50 *Life of Beethoven,* Thayer, ed. Forbes, Princeton U.P. 1967

52 *Jane Austen's Letters to her Sisters and others,* ed. Chapman, O.U.P. 1972, The Austen Papers, 1704–1856, John Rylands Library, Manchester

55 *Selected Letters of John Keats,* Doubleday, 1956

61 *Selected Letters of Sydney Smith,* O.U.P. 1953

63 *Berlioz: A Selection from his Letters,* ed. Seale, Gollancz, 1966

65 *Spoelberch de Levenjont collection*, quoted in *Lelia*, by André Maurois, Cape, 1953

67 *The Conduct of Love* by William Hazlitt, London, 1822

69 *Selected Letters of Edward Lear* by Vivien Noakes, O.U.P., 1988

72 The Letters of Queen Victoria, John Murray 1907 et seq: Advice to a Granddaughter by Richard Hough, Wm. Heinemann; Victoria R.I. by Elizabeth Longford, Weidenfeld & Nicolson, 1964

80 Mendelsohn: *An Introduction to his piano works*, ed. M. Halford, Alfred Pub Co.

81 *Bianchi, Life and Letters of Emily Dickinson*, Boston, 1924

82 *Letters from the House of Allcott*, ed. Bonstelle & Forest, Boston, 1914

85 *Letters of Victor Hugo*, ed. Meurice, Boston, 1896

89 *Letters of Mrs. Gaskell*, ed. J. Chaple & A. Pollard, Manchester University Press, 1966

92 *Letters of Lewis Carroll*, ed. M. Cohen, Macmillan, 1979

99 *Correspondence of Flaubert*, Gallimard-Pléiade, Paris, 18??

102 *Leicht zu Leben ohne Leichtsinn*, Letters ed. F.S. SeebassEckart-Verlag, Witten und Berlin, 1958. Translated by Marianne Obey

104 *Letters to Children*, ed. Eva G. Connor, Macmillan N.Y., 1938

109 *Letters of Anton Chekhov*, ed. Karlinsky & Heim, Harper & Row, 1973

111 *Marianne Thornton* by E.M. Forster, Edward Arnold, 1956

115 *The Letters of Mark Twain*, 3.v., University of California Press, 1992

118 *Englishmen at War, 1450–1900*, Books In, 1993

120 *Letters of William James*, Boston, 1920

124 *Winston Spencer Churchill* by Randolph Churchill Vol. One, Heinemann, 1966

128 *Letters of Robert Louis Stevenson*, ed. Colvin, Methuen, 1899

131 *Just Richmal* by Kay Williams, Genesis Pubs, 1986

133 Unpublished letter

135 *Gentleman Rider* by Alan Bishop, Michael Joseph, 1988

136 *Letters of Beatrix Potter*, ed. Judy Taylot, Warne 1929

138 previously unpublished letters

142 *O Beloved Kids*, Letters of Rudyard Kipling, ed. Gilbert, Weidenfeld & Nicolson, 1983

149 *Kenneth Grahame* by Patrick R. Chalmers, Methuen, 1933

150 *Debussy Letters* ed. Nichols & Lesure, Faber 1987

152 *Mountbatten*, by Philip Ziegler, 1985

157 *Letters of Jack London*, 1965

162 The Imperial War Museum

172 *Life and Letters of Walter Page* by Burton, Doubleday, 1924

175 The papers of R.A. Butler at Trinity College, Cambridge

178 *Congenial Spirits*, The Letters of Virginia Woolf, Volume, edited by Nigel Nicolson, Hogarth Press

180 *Yours, Plum*, the Letters of P.G. Wodehouse, Penguin 1992

183 *Portrait of a Marriage* by Nigel Nicolson, London, 1973

184 *Benjamin Britten, Letters from a Life*, ed. D. Mitchell & P. Reed, Faber & Faber, 1991

185 The Letters of D.H. Lawrence, Volume 6, Cambridge University Press

187 The Harry S. Truman Library

189 Unpublished letters of Conrad Potter Aiken

193 Letters of F. Scott Fitzgerald, ed. A. Turnbull, Bodley Head, 1964

196 Letters of J.R.R. Tolkien, ed. H. Carpenter, George Allen & Unwin, 1981

198 Letters of E.B. White, ed. D.L. Guth, Harper & Row, N.Y.

200 Last Letters Home, ed. T. Day-Lewis, Pan Macmillan, and Imperial War Museum 1995

205 Dwight D. Eisenhower Library, Abilene, Kansas

207 Francois Truffaut Letters, trans. G. Adair, Faber & Faber, 1989

209 Groucho Letters, Michael Joseph, 1967

211 Letters to Children by C.S. Lewis, Collins

215 *The Letters and Diaries of Evelyn Waugh*, Weidenfeld & Nicolson

222 *Gentleman Rider* by Alan Bishop, Michael Joseph, 1988: The Horse's Mouth by Joyce Cary, Michael Joseph, 1944

224 *Mr Thurber Regrets* . . . Little, Brown, Boston

226 Previously unpublished letter

229 *Kenneth Tynan Letters*, ed. Katheleen Tynan, Weidenfeld & Nicolson, 1994

234 *Days of Grace* by Arthur Ashe & Arnold Rampersand, Mandarin 1994: The Times, 29.6.93

237 Private letter drawing

243 Previously unpublished letter

INDEX OF WRITERS, WITH RECIPIENTS IN ITALICS